THE BIRTH OF Downtown Cleveland

The Birth of Downtown Cleveland

A Vision Interrupted

Dave Ford and Brad Schwartz

The History Press

Published by The History Press
Charleston, SC
www.historypress.com

First published 2018

Manufactured in the United States

ISBN 9781467140157

Library of Congress Control Number: 2018936082

Contents

Introduction

The focus and vision of Cleveland's central core, its "downtown," has changed many times since the area along the southern shore of Lake Erie was surveyed and mapped by the Connecticut Land Company in 1796. From its birth as a far outpost of the Connecticut Western reserve, Cleveland's downtown has been reborn time and again—from regional trading center to rail, trucking and air transportation hub and vital industrial manufacturing and economic center. Its current role is as a center for the development of high-tech industries. Even when the visions of its leaders and developers were interrupted by wars and economic and social downturns, Cleveland's forward-looking focus has enabled it to continually rebirth and retool itself to meet the needs of the world that surrounds it.

Cleveland, Ohio, became the great city that it is because of its location. Once described as being the "Best Location in the Nation," the city is sited at the mouth of a major river that empties into the center of America's Great Lakes. The Great Lakes are a unique and vital national and world asset, as they serve as a link between a rich, perfectly located United States–based manufacturing area and the Atlantic Ocean. Cleveland is located on the shores of Lake Erie, halfway between Buffalo, New York, and Detroit, Michigan, with the cities of Erie, Pennsylvania, and Toledo, Ohio, halfway between Buffalo and Detroit, respectively. The first Paleo-Indians set up seasonal camps in the region that surrounds the Cuyahoga River Valley about twelve thousand years ago, and while they benefited from the vast resources that they found in the area, they were also challenged by the same difficulties that would challenge future occupants of the area for many years—inherent swampiness and the associated diseases that accompany it.

When the first Caucasian settlers entered the region in 1796, more than ten thousand years after the first Native Americans did so, they came in search of a spot at the western reaches of the Connecticut Western Reserve—the eastern shores of the Cuyahoga River—where they could gain a foothold on a claim to an area that would give them access to vast resources before other foreign powers could do the same.

Cleveland has been a city on a seesaw since it was first incorporated as a village in the late 1700s and then as a city in 1836. The city has experienced times of great wealth and growth and times of poverty and decline. The city's location has always been its trump card. At its inception, its location allowed it to function as a conveniently located way station for the shipment of furs and other natural resources. In its heyday, its location allowed it to become one of the country's—and the world's—great industrial and manufacturing centers.

Through the years, Cleveland's primary challenge might have been that it usually went all-in with the cause du jour. Whether the city was working to become a center for steel manufacturing, chasing a dream of the world's finest manifestation of a design ethic or capitalizing on a new technology, Cleveland was continually going through cycles of profiting from a change and then failing from its decline.

The Cuyahoga River has literally been a lifeline throughout the city's history. Initially, the river served as a target for its first Caucasian settlers because it marked the western bounds of the Connecticut Western Reserve. As the city developed, the river served as a connection to the Great Lakes and to lands beyond them. Its shores served as a convenient means for loading goods manufactured in the city into lake steamers, as well as a place for offloading raw materials that the city used in its manufacturing processes. In the city's later years, the river would serve as a national bellwether for the environmental problems that accompanied America's industrial framework. After a series of instances where the toxic sludge that floated on the river caught fire, the river helped to spur the environmental movement in the United States.

Connecticut was one of several states that had land claims in the Ohio Country going back to the colonial period. Connecticut gave up most of its claims to the federal government so that the Northwest Territory could be created. However, it reserved the northeast corner of the territory for itself. This area came to be known as the Connecticut Western Reserve. As one of thirty-six founders of the Connecticut Land Company, General Moses Cleaveland was selected as one of its seven directors and was subsequently sent out as the company's agent to map and survey the company's holdings. In 1796, Cleaveland and his surveyors arrived at the mouth of the Cuyahoga River. General Cleaveland saw the land as an ideal location for the "capital city" of the Connecticut Western Reserve.

Even in its infancy, until it was able to establish itself as a center for Great Lakes shipping, the city went through periods of financial and population gains and losses. Nothing has shaped Cleveland's development more than transportation. Because of its midwestern location, Cleveland was in a prime spot for Great Lakes sail- and steamship-based commerce, an early hub for canal-based transportation and later a hub for east–west railroad lines. Cleveland's transportation network linked it to many of the world's great commercial centers. Cleveland's primary railroad era began in the late 1870s, when the New York Central and Nickel Plate Road built two major rail lines along Lake Erie's southern shoreline. This line linked New York with Chicago and St. Louis. The Valley Railway Line was chartered in 1871 to supply Cleveland's industrial plant with coal from southeast Ohio and West Virginia. Because of the extensive number of rail lines that transected the city, it needed to construct suitable terminals for the transfer of goods and passengers. Throughout its history, Cleveland would struggle with where to locate its Union Terminal, and that struggle continued to be a controversial topic that would lead to the creation and abandonment of large-scale development projects. Like many American cities, Cleveland swung back and forth politically and experienced both political and social greatness and political and social corruption and downfall.

Cleveland's first economic boom came during the Civil War years. Cleveland had become an industrial center by the mid-1800s and was able to manufacture many of the vital military goods that were needed by the Union army. By the end of the Civil War, Cleveland had grown into one of the five main oil refining centers in the United States. This was made possible by its proximity to the oil-rich areas of Western Pennsylvania and by the entrepreneurship of a few of its residents, such as John D. and William Rockefeller. The rise of Cleveland's prosperity brought along with it a sudden increase in population, as well as the rise of trade unions that worked to improve working and living conditions and increase workers' pay. The establishment of new industries in the late 1800s led to a more than doubling of its population. By the end of the 1870s, Cleveland had grown to a city with a population of more than 160,000.

The next thirty years were Cleveland's golden years, as the city prospered from technological innovation and expansion, as well as advances in culture. By the start of the new century, Cleveland's population had more than doubled to 382,000, making it the nation's seventh-largest city. In that same year, Cleveland's most popular mayor, Tom Johnson, was elected to the first of his four terms. Johnson was a visionary thinker, and his vision for Cleveland was built on big thoughts. A primary idea that was forwarded during his terms as mayor was that the city's future would be pinned to the development of a "Group Plan" that would be a central location for its governmental and civic functions. Over this same span of time, the city's economic prosperity was drawing people to it from all over the world, and Cleveland was becoming a city that was made up of many urban ethnic enclaves, each with its own language, foods, religions, music and cultural traditions.

In the early 1900s, Cleveland and other large industrial cities were overcome by overcrowding, poor living conditions, rampant crime, poverty and problems that were associated with the challenge of assimilating dissimilar populations. In an attempt to solve their urban problems, Cleveland, Chicago, Detroit and Washington, D.C., adopted the City Beautiful movement's new urban planning philosophy in the hope of creating new cities that were based on moral and civic virtue and social order. Cleveland's manifestation of the City Beautiful movement was seen in the Group Plan. The Group Plan was a design solution that was devised by an architecture and planning firm that was promoted by famed architects and planners Daniel Burnham, John M. Carrère and Arnold R. Brunner in response to Cleveland's Group Plan Commission's call for a "civic center" between Cleveland's New England–inspired Public Square and its lakefront. The Burnham group's 1903 plan was proposed to be a classic representation of City Beautiful thought—a modern, artificially lit grouping of Neoclassical civic buildings of uniform scale in height and mass, embracing an open civic area filled with grand fountains, sculptures and European-inspired formally planted areas reflective of the grounds of Europe's largest cities.

Cleveland has always had a "lakefront problem." The problem is associated with a desire to consolidate the city's railroad connections into a Union Terminal that in Burnham's plan was represented by a palatial "Union Station," located where the majority of Cleveland's rail lines were located—on the city's lakefront—at the northern terminus of a "Grand Mall." The extensive system of rail lines that ran east–west between the city and Lake Erie hampered the city's ability to take full advantage of the developmental opportunities that should have come with having access to an expansive lakeshore. Like most City Beautiful–inspired development projects, Cleveland's Group Plan project was originally proposed to take a generation to complete, and the world didn't stop changing while the city completed it. In the end, the completion of Cleveland's Group Plan project would be interrupted by two world wars, the Great Depression and ongoing changes in how the city's residents felt about the city and its downtown.

Burnham's Group Plan design for Cleveland has been lauded by some as being, on paper, the best embodiment to date of the City Beautiful movement's ideals. Cleveland made a good start in carrying out the construction of major elements of the plan. By 1930, a good number of the Group Plan's architectural elements had been constructed, but the loss of the plan's northern terminus gave it a lack of focus. To complicate the matter, in the first quarter of the twentieth century, Cleveland's industrial plant was prospering on the shoulders of its overworked citizens and its less fortunate citizens. At the same time, industrial production had been sparked by World War I, and the city was finding its cultural footing, thanks in large part to donations and endowments from its wealthiest citizens. These endowments would give rise to museums, cutting-edge healthcare facilities and world-class establishments that brought the arts to the city.

A critical blow to the Group Plan was manifested in the actions of two eccentric Cleveland brothers, Oris and Mantis Van Sweringen, who struck a "terminal" blow to the Group Plan's success while seeking to improve the chances of their plans to develop a suburban housing development east of Cleveland. By 1909, six years after the Group Plan was conceived, the brothers had assembled a large swath of land adjacent to Public Square to facilitate the development of a terminus for their transit line between Shaker Heights and downtown Cleveland—a project that would result in the construction of one of the world's tallest buildings, the Terminal Tower, which would stand over a Public Square–located Union Station. Their project caught the attention of Cleveland voters, who supported the project with the passage of a public referendum to develop a railway station in the Terminal Tower location and abandon the idea of a union terminal at the apex of Burnham's Great Mall. Like the city, the Terminal Tower development has seen good days and bad. In the late 1920s, as the Terminal Tower project was being completed, the Great Depression was looming, and the success of the Van Sweringen brothers and the city of Cleveland's future would be challenged.

The early twentieth century was a time of booms and busts for America's industrial cities, and these cities' fortunes and citizens became pawns of the period's ups and downs. During World War I, as many of Cleveland's citizens were dying in European fields, the economies of industrial cities were booming, with the cities growing at a remarkable rate. Modes of transportation changed from the horse and buggy to mechanized vehicles, which made it easier for many to flee the city and move to suburban locations.

Cleveland's industrial base has been a major shaper of its downtown. The city's factories were nestled up to its downtown area to receive raw materials from the Cuyahoga River. With Lake Erie to the north and the industrial belt of factories to the south of downtown, Cleveland's city center would follow the path of least resistance and grow east and west, using Euclid, Superior and Lakeside Avenues as conduits. There were also many small manufacturers that also needed labor. Printers, electroplaters, textiles workers, hat makers and the service industry created a great demand on the workforce. These small factories were spread throughout downtown buildings, contributing to the chaotic function of downtown as factories, garages, offices and residences all comingled in an unsupervised quilt.

Industrial jobs and a promise of wealth created an irresistible pull on European immigrants and on the rural southern population. This contributed to the creation of Cleveland's many ethnic neighborhoods. Cleveland's employment history has thrived and failed according to the economic stresses that were faced by Cleveland and other industrial cities. As the Great Depression took hold of the world, a groundswell of discontent among the less fortunate was matched by trouble at the top when their bill came due. Much of the nation's industrial and civic development had been leveraged against stock holdings, which grew rapidly until a series of checks to stock overvaluation occurred in the late 1920s, and when the stock market crashed, projects that had been based on artificially high stock valuations crashed along with them. By 1931, two years after the Great Depression officially began, half of Cleveland's workers were unemployed.

The Great Lakes Exposition was held in Cleveland, Ohio, during the Great Depression summers of 1936 and 1937. The purpose of the exposition was to commemorate the centennial of Cleveland's incorporation as a city in 1836 and celebrate the industrial riches of the Great Lakes states. The exposition was organized by a small group of Cleveland business leaders who in just four months raised $1.1 million in loaned investments to develop the exposition grounds. There was little time to pull the exposition together, and in just eighty days, thousands of Cleveland's building trade workers and additional hundreds of men who were employed through the federal government's Works Progress Administration completed the work of installing utilities, paving roads and plazas and constructing the exposition's more than 150 buildings and features.

A historical plus for the city was that for the duration of the exposition—and for the first time in its history—Cleveland's downtown and its lakefront were linked by a wooden causeway built over the lakeshore railroad frontage that had been separated since the rail lines were laid down fifty years earlier. Cleveland's Great Lakes Science Center, the Rock and Roll Hall of Fame and Museum, the Cleveland Browns' First Energy Field and Burke Lakefront Airport now occupy the land where the exposition stood during the summers of 1936 and 1937. The 1940s were again prosperous times in America's cities, but problems that were fostered before and during the Depression persisted, including increasing racial tensions and the flight of Caucasian residents to the suburbs. Cleveland's prosperity in the 1940s brought even more people to the city, and by 1950, Cleveland's population had risen to an all-time high of 915,000.

Until its recent retooling as a center for medical and technical research, Cleveland's health was always measured by the vitality of its industrial and manufacturing sectors—the most important of which were the manufacturing of iron and steel products—as well as the city's ability to deliver those goods to the marketplace.

Following the end of World War II, many of Cleveland's industries were able to retool their production lines and turn over to manufacturing the types of domestic products that would be needed by America's families during the postwar baby boom, including homes, automobiles and home appliances. This trend continued in the postwar housing boom, which saw tens of thousands of new homes constructed in suburban areas for new families who sought cleaner and greener neighborhoods away from the soot and smoke created by the ring of factories and mills around downtown Cleveland. These new suburban neighborhoods were outside the reach of the city's interurban rail lines and streetcar lines, but advancements were made in the production of automobiles and buses, giving suburb dwellers the means to access the goods they needed from newly developed and convenient shopping centers.

Cleveland is a restless city that has always had big ambitions. From the first glimmers of the Group Plan in 1903 until the present, its citizens have been creating plans to make the city a better place to live. It is not a city prone to remaining static and does not resist change. With heavy industry waning in the United States, this Rust Belt city has been busy trying to redefine itself. To move forward, it requires a vision that would adjust to the needs of its citizens and the demands of industry. The efforts to adjust and improve are just as difficult and tumultuous in the present as the changes the city made at the turn of the prior century. The key to a successful future for Cleveland is keeping its most valuable assets, its people, in the city.

The 1970s marked the low point of the city on many fronts. During that dark decade, Cleveland lost 23.6 percent of its population, far more than the national average. It became the first major American city since the Great Depression to default on its loans. Highways cut through neighborhoods, ripping apart the fabric of many solid communities. The Cuyahoga River had become famous for its 1969 fire, and Lake Erie was slowly dying. At some point, a city hits bottom. All these events in one way or another forced people to consider change in the city. The transformation of Cleveland's downtown was not going to be quick. Over the years, committees were formed, surveys were conducted and collated and action has been taken. In recent years, the desire to revive downtown Cleveland in an interesting and livable way has taken on a life of its own. The results of all the information gathering has drawn interest in improving housing, shopping options, restaurants, more green space, transportation and new employment opportunities.

Unlike the original Group Plan, a holistic approach is being used to create a truly forward-looking and hopefully permanent process to the rejuvenation of downtown. In the 2000 census, the population of Cleveland was 476,000, and by 2010, it had dropped 17 percent to 396,000. Fortunately, since 2010, the population has stabilized at about 385,000 people. This stabilization has hopefully signaled a turnaround in the fortunes of the city. Downtown Cleveland is uniquely poised to use its existing town center to create that desirable, livable, residential shopping experience. Developers have taken notice and are leveraging the potential of downtown Cleveland. They are taking strides toward creating a unique, vibrant downtown experience. An important keystone to the future success of downtown Cleveland is creating an attractive residential core of hotels, apartments and condominiums. Downtown developers and the city are focusing on key areas to create thriving residential and commercial environments in the immediate downtown area. Downtown Cleveland is now the fastest-growing neighborhood in Northeast Ohio. In 2017, more than 17,000 residents live in downtown Cleveland, and retail investment is creating a welcoming and comfortable place to live and work.

Cleveland's Group Plan Commission is still actively developing the area that was the focus of Burnham's original 1903 plan. The commission's efforts to revive and develop Cleveland's downtown core has resulted in the development of Cleveland's lakefront and Public Square. Cleveland's lakefront is probably the most improved of all its downtown areas. The lakefront hosts an impressive array of world-class attractions, including First Energy Stadium, the Great Lakes Science Center and the Rock and Roll Hall of Fame and Museum. Restaurants, retail arcade, office space and even possible apartments are planned for the area near the Ninth Street Pier north of the Hall of Fame. The city of Cleveland is poised to meet the future, and its downtown and its neighborhoods are experiencing a new period of vitality and growth.

Authors' note: This book is set up as a collection of five essays that explore "Visions" that have shaped the development of Cleveland and its downtown. Because of this book's narrow focus, some development issues are addressed in more than one chapter, although the treatments of those issues vary in how they are addressed. While the focus of this book is on the historical development of Cleveland's downtown, the book also discusses other factors that influenced its development.

Early Cleveland

Geography has made us neighbors. History has made us friends.
—John F. Kennedy

Cleveland, Ohio, became the great city that it is because it is located at the mouth of a major river that empties into America's Great Lakes. America's Great Lakes are a unique and vital national and world asset because they serve as a link between a rich, perfectly located United States–based manufacturing area and the Atlantic Ocean. Cleveland is located on the shores of Lake Erie, halfway between Buffalo, New York, and Detroit, Michigan, with the cities of Erie, Pennsylvania, and Toledo, Ohio, halfway between Buffalo and Detroit, respectively.

When the first Paleo-Indians set up seasonal camps in the region that surrounds the Cuyahoga River Valley after the Wisconsin Glacier retreated to the north about twelve thousand years ago, their small bands of nomadic hunting and foraging groups benefited from the vast natural resources that the region offered, and they were challenged by the region's vast wetlands. These seasonal groups of Paleo and "Archaic Indians" never established a permanent civilization in the Cuyahoga River Valley but instead remained regular seasonal residents who eventually established systems of long-distance trade with Native Americans throughout the Great Lakes Region and to the south and west.

When the first Caucasian settlers entered the region in 1796, more than ten thousand years after the first Native Americans, they came in search of a spot at the western reaches of the Connecticut Western Reserve—the eastern shores of the Cuyahoga River—where they could gain a foothold on a claim to an area that would give them access to vast resources before other foreign powers could do the same. This party of venture capitalists was faced with the same promise of riches and the same challenges that the region's natural features had presented to Native Americans for more than ten thousand years. Settlers and entrepreneurs would take advantage of the region's assets and work hard to tame and overcome the negative aspects.

Primitive transportation in the Great Lakes Region was by foot. East–west transportation was along the sandy ridges that were left behind by retreating glaciers, and north–south transportation was along river valleys and gorges that had been carved by advancing glaciers.

The Great Lakes

America's current Great Lakes and their shorelines were formed by the advance and retreat of glaciers during the last ice age, which started about thirty-one thousand years ago. The ice sheet expanded for more than thirteen thousand years before the earth's temperatures warmed and it began its melt-back period. It took another seven thousand years for the glacier's ice to fully retreat to a point north of Wisconsin. This glaciation period is known as the Wisconsin Glaciation. The mile-thick glacier scoured the areas of what is now the watershed that includes the Michigan peninsulas, western Wisconsin and Minnesota and the northern portions of Indiana and Ohio, as well as the New York panhandle and Southern Ontario. All rivers and streams in these areas drain into the Great Lakes, which in turn flow eastward through the St. Lawrence River into the Atlantic Ocean.

Flow through the Great Lakes starts from the west and moves east. The water from the two upper great lakes of Superior and Michigan flows through the St. Mary's River and the Straight of Mackinaw (in the state of Michigan) into Lake Huron. This water then moves into Lake Erie through the St. Claire and Detroit Rivers. The waters from Lake Erie then drain through the Niagara River into Lake Ontario, and then they flow into the Atlantic Ocean through the St. Lawrence River.

A Great Lakes system existed in North America before the Wisconsin Glaciation, but its configuration was somewhat different, with the major differences being in the connection between Lake Huron and Lake Erie.

Before the Wisconsin Glaciation, water from the Superior, Michigan and Huron lake basins flowed into the area that is now occupied by the Georgian Bay off Lake Huron. From there it flowed through the area that is now the Trent River to the Bay of Quinte on Lake Ontario. Before the last glaciation period, southeast Michigan and Northern Ohio and Indiana were drained by the Erigan River (pre-glacial, no longer exists), which flowed through the area that is now covered by Lake Erie and Lake Ontario and then out to sea through the St. Lawrence Basin.

LAKE ERIE BECOMES THE OLDEST GREAT LAKE

The advance of the Wisconsin Glacier moved in several lobes through the region. As they are today, the surface rocks of the Great Lakes region were made up of shales, salts and sandstones, and the glacier followed a path of least resistance through the area where these surface rocks were the softest. The glacier was divided into lobes by following this path along pre-glaciation river valleys. The glacier's ice eventually moved out of the St. Lawrence watershed and into the Mississippi watershed but stopped short of the Ohio River to the south.

About 14,500 years ago, the glacier's ice went through cycles of retreat and advance and created a moraine in what are today Northern Indiana and Southern Michigan that in turn formed a natural dam, stopping rising water that was being created by the melting of the glacier from flowing south into the Mississippi watershed. Coupled with this, the glacier's weight had depressed the level of the area in Northern Indiana and Ohio. As the lobes shrank back into the valleys that directed their flow, the increased meltwater, combined with the damming of that water by the moraine, formed Lake Erie and Lake Ontario. The cycle of glacial advance and retreat continued for thousands of years, eventually lowering the lower great lakes' basins to their current level.

EARLY NATIVE AMERICAN SETTLEMENTS

Following the retreat of the glaciers and the formation of the current Great Lakes system about ten to twelve thousand years ago, Native Americans moved into the region and created a number of small encampments along the shores of the Great Lakes. The early Native American settlers of the area followed sandy ridges that had been created by the glacial advance and retreat—the same ridges that today are the pathways of important east–west highways. Nearly three thousand years ago, the Adena and Hopewell Mound Builder people moved into and populated the Northeast Ohio region.

Through the centuries, these Native American people developed agriculture-based communities and created more permanent and stationary civilizations. These people began to live year-round in large, fortified villages; grew corn, beans and squash; and hunted animals for their meat and for their fur. Because these people now relied on maintaining "their land," they experienced conflict over landownership with competing tribes, which resulted in the loss of many lives and the shifting of landownership from one tribe to another. To escape the ongoing intertribal conflict in the Northeast Ohio area, several tribes within the Ottawa Nation moved west into the Maumee and Sandusky Bay areas, moving the fur trade farther west along the Lake Erie shoreline. Following subsequent early woodland Native American settlements in the region between 500 BC and AD 100 and Middle Woodland settlements between AD 100 and AD 700, a period of increased ceremonial and material exchange between Lake Erie–area Native Americans and Native Americans outside the Lake Erie area flourished and expanded the ranges of trade and ceremonial exchange. The results of this expanded trade included the appearance of sophisticated decorated pottery and artistic items in the local historic record.

The Midwest Native American cultures, including the Adena culture, also began building large ceremonial mounds, some in large concentrations. These mounds were found in their greatest concentrations in southern Ohio, but they are also found in northern Summit County. Additional evidence of widespread fist-century trade by Cuyahoga Valley–area Native Americans include the presence of projectile points, flint-blade knives and ceramics from the Hopewell culture. In a mound south of Brecksville, Ohio—twenty miles to the south of Cleveland—a cache of trade goods from outside the Cuyahoga Valley area was found within a six-sided stone crypt. A smaller mound between Willowick and Eastlake, Ohio (twenty miles to the east of Cleveland), was found to contain ceremonial spear points made from stone that is found in the state of Illinois—all signs of a wide range of trade with civilizations from outside the Lake Erie area.

Mound building in the Cuyahoga Valley area ceased after AD 400 and was replaced with an expansion of Native American settlements to river valleys that paralleled the Cuyahoga to the east and west. An agricultural base and the use of storage pits in their homes allowed people from these cultures to persist in the area year-round. Also found in these settlements were more complex tools and ornaments made of antler and bone. During the spring, people lived in camps along the lakeshore ridges, along ponds and bogs or around headwaters of creeks, where they collected plants and fished.

From 1200 to 1600, outside influences on local cultures from Meso-America and Mississippian cultures were seen, including the construction of new building styles and the introduction of new foods and the use of materials that were traded for with Native American cultures from south of the Ohio River. This influence was even stronger within the Fr. Ancient group, probably ancestors of later Shawnees. Between 1300 and 1500, Lake Erie Native American villages became larger, with rectangular-shaped buildings and fortress-like constructions.

Beginning around 1500, a period of wars between competing tribes reduced the number of Cuyahoga Valley–area Native American villages. It is possible that these warlike cultures were spurred by competition for scarcer resources as a result of the "Little Ice Age" that began around AD 1500. Colder temperatures caused nutritional deficiencies and disease, and the regional population continuously declined until around 1640; the Cleveland-area region became virtually uninhabited from 1640 to 1740. Word of extensive trade, followed by the relative abandonment of the Lake Erie shoreline by Native American tribes, attracted European settlers to the area who had moved farther and farther west after establishing their first settlements in the New World in the early 1600s.

As often was the case, the first Caucasian settlers to enter the Cuyahoga Valley were a group of Moravian missionaries, who established Pilgerruh, a Native American missionary settlement in the Cuyahoga Valley. Pilgerruh, or Pilgrim's Rest, was the first organized settlement in the Cleveland area. Located in the Cuyahoga Valley, Pilgerruh was established in 1786 by Moravian missionaries and their Indian converts. They were led by Reverend John Heckewelder and Reverend David Zeisberger, who had been involved in the 1772 settlements of Schoenbrunn, which was the first organized settlement in Ohio, and Gnadenhutten in the Tuscarawas Valley. The missionaries, who were driven out of the Tuscarawas Valley area by the British during the Revolutionary War, moved west to the Detroit area and established a settlement on the Huron River. In 1786, Congress awarded lands in the Tuscarawas Valley to them, but hostilities from neighboring tribes prevented their return to that area and instead they moved into the

Cuyahoga Valley area, where they constructed a group of buildings on the ruins of an old Ottawa Indian village. One year later, the Moravian missionaries left Pilgerruh and headed west to establish the New Salem encampment near Milan, Ohio.

THE CUYAHOGA RIVER

The Cuyahoga River meanders through the Cuyahoga Valley and feeds into Lake Erie. The river is Cleveland's river, and each year, thousands of ore boats and cargo ships enter Cleveland's port through the mouth of the Cuyahoga River and empty their contents at offloading stations along the river's shore. The river was one of the features along which the "Greenville Treaty Line" ran beginning in 1795—per the Treaty of Greenville, which ended the Northwest Indian War in the Ohio Country—effectively becoming the western boundary of the United States and remaining so briefly. The river is famous for having been so polluted in the late 1960s that it caught fire. This sad event helped to spur the environmental movement in the United States. The name Cuyahoga is derived either from the Mohawk Indian word *Cayagaga*, meaning "crooked river," or from the Seneca Indian word *Cuyahoga*, meaning "place of the jawbone."

The 100-mile-long Cuyahoga River originates to the east of Cleveland in Geauga County, where it first flows southward to Akron, Ohio, and Cuyahoga Falls and then turns north and flows through the Cuyahoga Valley National Park in northern Summit County and southern Cuyahoga County. It then flows through Independence, Valley View, Cuyahoga Heights, Newburgh Heights and Cleveland and empties into Lake Erie. The Cuyahoga River watershed drains 813 square miles land in Northern Ohio.

The Cuyahoga River was formed by the advance and retreat of ice sheets during the Wisconsin Glaciation. The final glacial retreat about ten to twelve thousand years ago caused river, which originally flowed south, to switch direction and flow to the north. As the river carved its way around glacial debris left by the receding ice sheet, it took on its winding U-shaped path. The river's origin is only thirty miles from its terminus, but its meandering pathway stretches its length to one hundred miles. Along most of its length, the depth of the river averages between three to six feet. Closer to the lake, the river becomes wider and deeper. At points farther away from the lake, the river's depth and width are maintained by dredging and piling along its shore. In the 1970s, a group of researchers at Kent State University reported:

> *The surface is covered with a brown oily film observed upstream as far as the Southerly Plant effluent. In addition, large quantities of black heavy oil floating in slicks, sometimes several inches thick, are observed frequently. Debris and trash are commonly caught up in these slicks forming an unsightly floating mess. Anaerobic action is common as the dissolved oxygen is seldom above a fraction of a part per million. The discharge of cooling water increases the temperature by 10 to 15 °F* [5.6 to 8.3 °C]. *The velocity is negligible, and sludge accumulates on the bottom. Animal life does not exist. The color changes from gray-brown to rusty brown as the river proceeds downstream. This entire reach is grossly polluted.*

At least thirteen fires have been reported on the Cuyahoga River, the first occurring in 1868. The largest river fire in 1952 caused more than $1 million in damage to boats, a bridge and a riverfront office building.

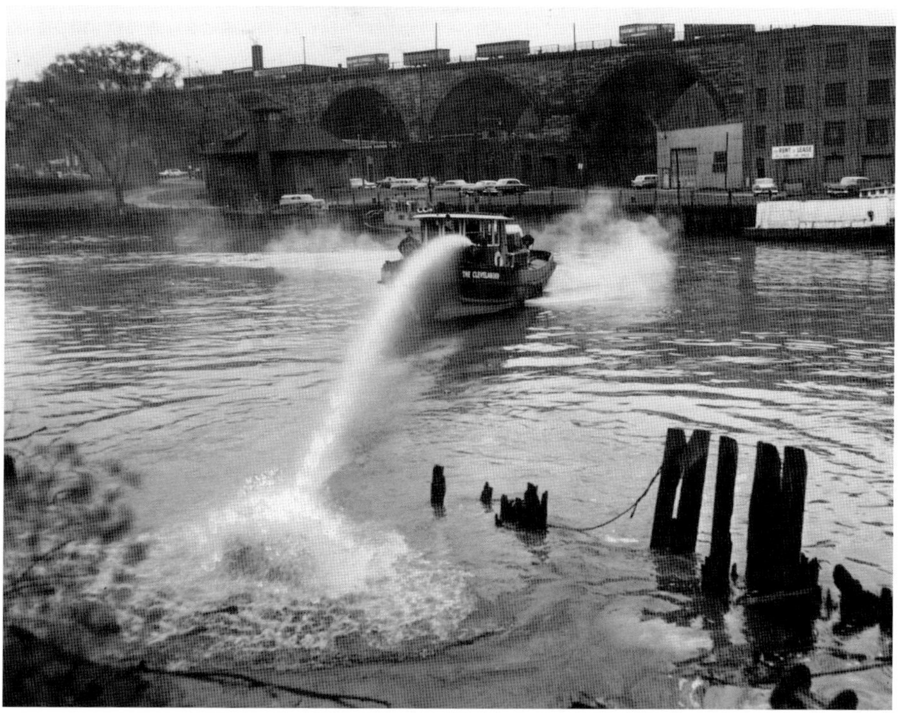

A fireboat breaks up an oil slick on the Cuyahoga River in Cleveland's industrial flats section in 1961. *Cleveland Memory Project.*

The 1969 river fire was reported in *TIME* magazine, which described the Cuyahoga as "the river that oozes rather than flows" and in which a person "does not drown but decays." Because the smaller 1969 fire didn't last long enough for anyone to take photographs of it, the pictures that were displayed in the 1969 *TIME* magazine article were from the more dangerous and costly 1952 fire.

The 1969 Cuyahoga River fire did much good, though, as it helped to spur a movement of water pollution control actions that resulted in the Clean Water Act, the Great Lakes Water Quality Agreement and the creation of the federal Environmental Protection Agency. The Great Lakes Brewing Company of Cleveland also named its Burning River Pale Ale after the event. Water quality has improved, and partially in recognition of this improvement, the Cuyahoga River was designated one of fourteen American Heritage Rivers in 1998.

Originally, the river emptied into a shallow marsh along the lake, about four thousand feet west of its current mouth. Its current mouth just west of downtown Cleveland is man-made, affording shipping traffic to flow freely between the river and the lake. The navigable portion of the river along its last five miles is periodically dredged by the U.S. Army Corps of Engineers to maintain the river at a depth of twenty-seven feet. This allows Great Lakes freighter traffic to unload ore, asphalt, gravel, petroleum, salt, steel and other products at receiving and processing plants along the lower Cuyahoga River banks in Cleveland's Flats District. The Corps of Engineers has also straightened river banks and widened turning basins in the Federal Navigation Channel on the lower Cuyahoga River to facilitate maritime operations.

The Firelands was part of the Western Reserve of Connecticut in the Northwest Territory. In 1786, Connecticut ceded most of its western lands to the U.S. government in preparation for the Northwest Ordinance of 1787. The state kept its claim to an area of land in the northeastern portion of the Northwest Territory known as the Connecticut Western Reserve. Connecticut chose to sell most of the land in the Western Reserve to finance the state's educational system. About 500,000 acres were reserved for Connecticut citizens who had suffered property losses during the American Revolution.

The Connecticut Western Reserve

Connecticut was one of several states that had land claims in the Ohio Country going back to the colonial period. Connecticut gave up most of its claims to the federal government so that the Northwest Territory could be created. However, it reserved the northeast corner of the territory for itself. This area came to be known as the Connecticut Western Reserve. The Western Reserve had two parts. The western part of the region was known as the Firelands. The state gave plots of land in this area to people who had lost their property in the American Revolution. The Connecticut government sold the eastern portion of the reserve to the Connecticut Land Company in 1795. The $1.2 million earned through the land sale was spent on public education in the state of Connecticut. This portion of the Western Reserve became known as the Firelands, or the Sufferers' Lands. During the Revolution, British troops had burned several Connecticut towns, and many of their residents had lost everything they owned. They were able to start over again in the Northwest Territory. A company called the Ohio Corporation distributed the land to eligible applicants. Much of the settlement of the region did not occur until after the War of 1812.

Moses Cleaveland Surveys the Cuyahoga Valley

As one of thirty-six founders of the Connecticut Land Company, General Moses Cleaveland was selected as one of its seven directors and was subsequently sent out as the company's agent to map and survey the company's holdings. In 1796, Cleaveland and his surveyors arrived at the mouth of the Cuyahoga River. Cleaveland quickly saw the land, which had previously belonged to Native Americans, as an ideal location for the "capital city" of the Connecticut Western Reserve. Cleaveland and his surveyors quickly began making plans for the new city. He paced out a nine-and-a-half-acre Public Square, similar to those in New England. His surveyors decided on the name Cleaveland, after their leader. In October, Cleaveland and his staff returned to Connecticut, where he pursued his ambition in political, military and law affairs, never once returning to the settlement he established.

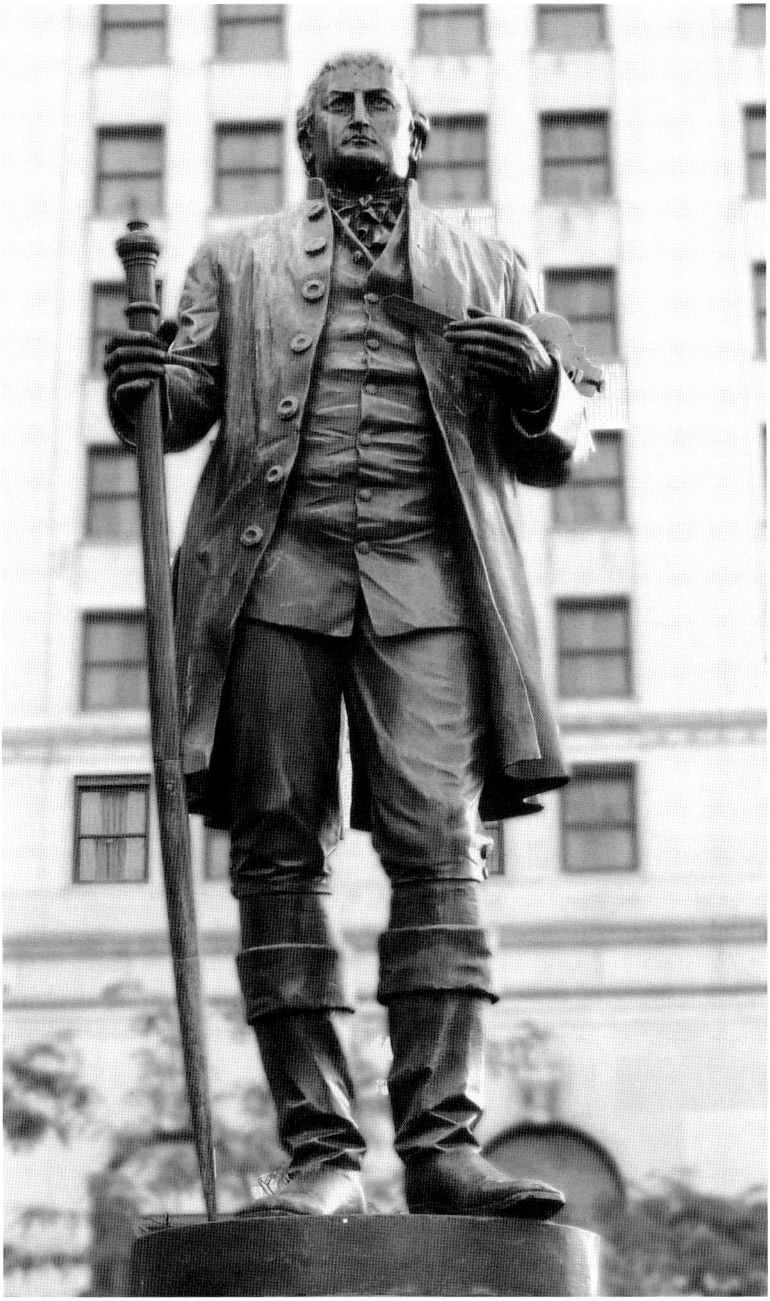

This eight-foot tall bronze of Moses Cleaveland stands on Cleveland's Public Square in honor of the man who led the first expedition of the Connecticut Land Company to the mouth of the Cuyahoga River at the western extent of the Connecticut Western Reserve in 1796. *Ford.*

Schoolteachers Job Phelps Stiles (born circa 1769 in Granville, Massachusetts) and his wife, Talitha Cumi Elderkin (born in 1779 in Hartford, Connecticut), were two of only three original settlers who stayed there over the first winter of 1796–97 when, attended by Seneca Native American women, Talitha Cumi gave birth to Charles Phelps Stiles, the first white child born in the Western Reserve. They lived at first on Lot 53, the present corner of Superior Avenue and West Third Street adjacent to the Terminal Tower, but later moved southeast to higher ground in Newburgh, Ohio, to escape malarial conditions in the lower Cuyahoga Valley.

CLEVELAND TAKES SHAPE

Development of the area occurred quickly after 1800. In 1802, it was reported in the first area census that there were seventy-six free males over the age of twenty-one in the Cleaveland area. This population was fortified by the construction of the first distillery in the area in the year 1800. In the same year, Cleaveland became part of the newly formed Trumbull County. Ohio was admitted to the Union in 1803, and then the U.S. Mail Service extended to Cleveland. In 1805, Cleaveland was reallocated to Geauga County, and one of the area's first settlers, Lorenzo Carter, built the *Zephyr*, which became the first ship to be launched from Cleaveland's shores. In 1810, Cuyahoga County was formed, and Cleaveland—whose population had dropped to fifty-seven persons—became its county seat. In 1813, the Battle of Lake Erie and Oliver Hazard Perry's victory at Put-in-Bay Island—part of the War of 1812—shook early Lake Erie shoreline residents. In the same year, the first county courthouse was constructed in Cleaveland, and the Village of Cleaveland was incorporated on December 23, 1814.

Further change and progress occurred in the Cleaveland area between 1815 and 1820. Alfred Kelley was elected first president of the Village of Cleaveland, the *Walk-in-the-Water* became the first Great Lakes–based steamship to serve Cleaveland and the area's first newspaper, the *Cleaveland Gazette and Commercial Register*, began to be published. In 1819, the *Cleveland Herald and Gazette* published its first issue for the village's six hundred residents—dropping the *a* from the paper's banner to allow it to fit within the allowed space.

TRANSPORTATION SHAPES CLEVELAND'S FUTURE

In 1825, the federal government recognized the need to improve travel in the mid-western portion of the country, and construction of the Ohio and Erie Canal followed the construction of the Erie Canal in New York and Pennsylvania. The Ohio and Erie Canal opened better trade routes south to the Akron area in 1827 and, eventually, farther south to the Ohio River. The canal's establishment of an effective means of transportation from Cleveland south to the Ohio River opened trade routes for Ohio's fledgling cities all the way to the Gulf of Mexico.

It can be safely said that nothing shaped Cleveland's development more than transportation. Because of its mid-western location, Cleveland was in a prime spot to be an important port for Great Lakes sail and steamship-based commerce, an early hub for canal-based transportation and, later, a hub for east–west railroad lines. The country's vast canal system was a revolutionary system of commerce and trade that fueled America's rapid growth in the 1820s and 1830s. The regional canals built in the early nineteenth century

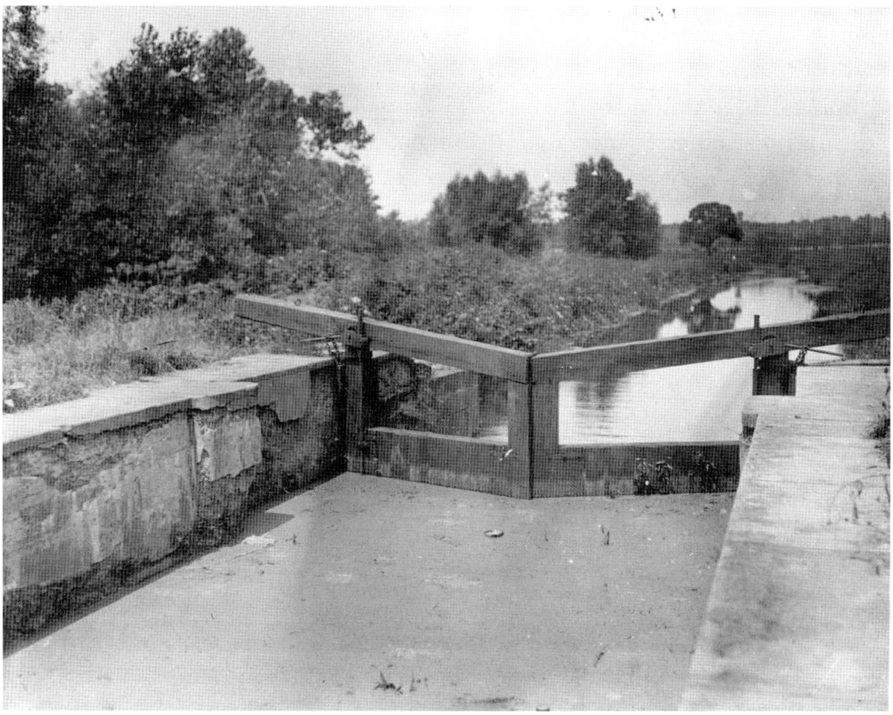

Modern view of a double water level lock on the Ohio and Erie Canal at Forty-Ninth Street, across from Canal Road, in Cleveland, Ohio. *Cleveland Memory Project.*

developed into an interconnected national network of waterways. Canals in northeast and Midwest states linked the Atlantic Ocean to the Gulf of Mexico, and the Ohio and Erie Canal linked Cleveland to the interior of Ohio and to southern and eastern states. The canal system also fueled westward expansion and the national market economy that accompanied it. Between 1825 and 1847, 813 miles of canals were constructed across Ohio. Generally, America's canal era lasted from 1790 to 1860, with most of America's canals being built over a thirty-year period from 1820 to 1850.

THE RAILROAD BECOMES KING

Cleveland's primary railroad era began in the late 1870s, when the New York Central and Nickel Plate Road built two major rail lines along Lake Erie's southern shoreline. This line was intended to link New York with Chicago and St. Louis. The Valley Railway Line was chartered in 1871 to supply Cleveland's industrial plant with coal from southeast Ohio and West Virginia. Construction of the rail line began in 1878, and operations started between Cleveland and Canton in 1880. In 1882, the line was extended to Wheeling, West Virginia.

Railroad service to and through Cleveland continued through the city's lakeshore railroad terminals until the Cleveland Union Terminal Project was conceived by the Van Sweringen brothers in about 1920. The brothers owned the Nickel Plate Railroad and the Chesapeake and Ohio Railroads. The Cleveland Union Terminal project was conceived to bring the railroads into Cleveland's Public Square instead of to the Lake Erie shoreline, which was a benefit to the Nickel Plate Railroad because it kept that line on the higher ground. The Pennsylvania Railroad that ran between Cleveland and Pittsburgh stayed out of the Union Terminal project and retained its original lines. The Union Terminal line used overhead trolley engines to move railroad cars from Cleveland's east side to its west side through its downtown terminal. In this system, railroad cars would be disconnected from their steam engines and connected to the "cleaner and quieter" electric engines east of Cleveland and would eventually be reconnected to steam engines west of Cleveland after they had made the seventeen-mile trip through the city.

The Cleveland Union Terminal had a total of thirty-seven tracks that serviced the Van Sweringen brothers' Shaker Rapid Transit lines, which

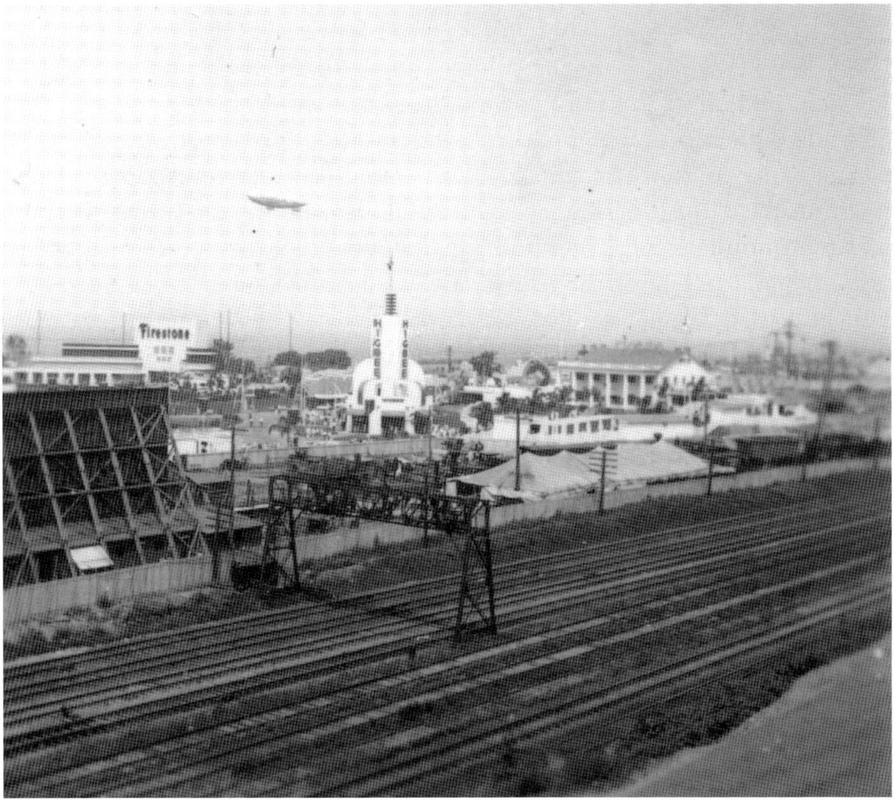

View of Cleveland's lakefront in 1936, looking north over the eight-track expanse of Cleveland's lakeshore railway system, with elements of the Great Lakes Exposition. *Schwartz.*

were used for special trains for public events and passenger cars, such as the "Pullman Line," as well as freight and mail car lines, which were used to shuttle rail cars through Cleveland. The terminal also included service lines that were used to house and service railroad cars. These lines totaled 190 miles of track in and around downtown Cleveland. Eventually, the Erie Railroad built a 300-mile rail line from Cleveland to Pittsburgh that connected with the Cleveland Union Terminal lines, and then the Wheeling & Lake Erie Railroad built a rail line that connected Cleveland to Canton to the southeast. Other rail lines joined in the project, and soon the project included 960 miles of track.

CLEAVELAND BECOMES CLEVELAND

In 1829, a need for a public market and lakeshore lighthouse was seen to serve Cleaveland's population of 1,075, and in 1830, the *Cleveland Advertiser* dropped the *a* from the village's name to allow the newspaper's name to fit on its masthead. The village wasn't immune to problems, with the area's continuing problem with boggy conditions contributing to a cholera epidemic in 1832 that killed fifty village residents.

In 1836, Cleveland and its sister city just across the Cuyahoga River, Ohio City, were incorporated as cities. John Willey was elected Cleveland's first mayor, and Josiah Barber was elected as Ohio City's first mayor. Willey and a group of other residents bought a section of Cleveland's Flats area adjacent to the Cuyahoga River with plans to transform it into Cleveland Centre, a business and residential district. Willey then bought a piece of land from the southeast section of Ohio City across from Columbus Street in Cleveland. Willey named the new development Willeyville and then built the Columbus Street Bridge, which connected the two sections. Willey's bridge redirected commercial traffic to Cleveland before it could reach Ohio City's business district, which angered Ohio City residents and caused a rivalry between Ohio City and Cleveland.

Ohio City residents lobbied for a second bridge to be built to allow traffic to return to Ohio City, and in late 1836, they tried to stop the use of Willey's bridge by bombing the Ohio City end of it. The explosives caused only minor damage, so a group of one thousand Ohio City volunteers dug deep ditches at both ends of the bridge, making it impossible for horses and wagons to reach the bridge. The conflict escalated to Ohio City residents showing up at the bridge brandishing guns, crowbars, axes and other weapons. They were met by Willey and a group of armed Cleveland citizens. A battle between the two groups broke out on the bridge and resulted in two men being seriously wounded before the county sheriff arrived to end the violence and arrest some of the combatants. A court injunction prevented further bloodshed and led to an end to the conflict. Ohio City was eventually annexed by Cleveland in 1854.

The Columbus Street Bridge became an important asset for Cleveland, permitting produce to enter the city from the surrounding hinterlands and helping to expand the city's mercantile base. This was greatly increased with the coming of the Ohio and Erie Canal, which realized the city's potential as a major Great Lakes port. Later, as a halfway point for iron ore coming from Minnesota across the Great Lakes and for coal and other raw materials coming by rail from the south, Cleveland became one of the major manufacturing and population centers of the United States and was home to numerous major steel firms.

By 1839, Cleveland had become the nation's forty-fifth-largest city, with a population of more than six thousand. With the city's rapid growth following the construction of the Ohio and Erie Canal and increased steamer traffic on Lake Erie bringing wealth from the eastern and western ends of the Great Lakes region, Cleveland changed from a small local asset to an important national location. With this change came the establishment of the Cleveland Medical College in 1843 and the chartering of the Cleveland Library Association and the laying of the cornerstone for the St. John Cathedral in 1848. By 1849, Cleveland's population had rapidly grown to more than seventeen thousand and Cuyahoga County's population had risen to nearly fifty thousand.

The 1850s saw Cleveland's transformation into a cultural destination, with the establishment of the Cleveland Ladies Temperance Union and Cleveland's fist opera performance. In 1856, the city's water distribution system began to offer service; in 1857, the city's Omnibus service began; and in 1858, its first sewer was constructed.

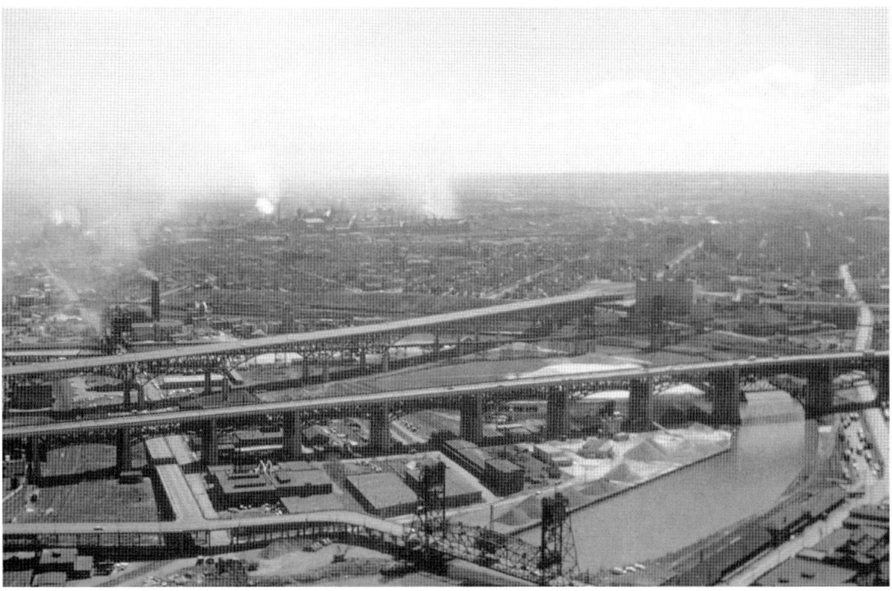

An aerial view of bridges over the north end of the Cuyahoga River, looking toward Cleveland's industrial flats section, adjacent to the city's downtown area. *Cleveland Memory Project.*

The 1860s brought political and social change to the city when Abraham Lincoln won 58 percent of the vote in nine of eleven wards for the presidency in 1860. In 1861, as the threat of Southern secession became more likely, competing rhetoric in Cleveland's newspapers became more heated. The *Herald* celebrated Lincoln's victory as one of right over wrong, of Unionists over secession-minded Southern Democrats, while the *Leader* dismissed threats of the South's secession. The *Plain Dealer*, meanwhile, argued that secession was imminent. When war broke out in April 1861, Cleveland Democrats and Republicans decided to end their dispute and united to form the Union Party to support Lincoln's war effort.

The Civil War years brought an economic boom to Cleveland. The city was making the transition from a small town to an industrial giant. Railroad iron and gun-carriage axles were being manufactured in Cleveland for civilian and military use. The city's garment industry began to prosper, and by 1863, more than one-fifth of the U.S. Navy's ships that were intended for use on the Great Lakes were being built in Cleveland. By 1865, that figure had increased to 44 percent. In addition, food, blankets and reading material were provided by citizens to recruits at Cleveland-area military camps before they were made available through government stores.

CLEVELAND GROWS UP

By the end of the American Civil War, Cleveland was one of the five main oil refining centers in the United States (besides Pittsburgh, Philadelphia, New York City and the region in northwestern Pennsylvania) where most of the oil originated. Standard Oil began as a partnership based in Cleveland among John D. Rockefeller, William Rockefeller, Henry M. Flagler and Samuel Andrews. Cleveland's prosperity during the Civil War had drawn many to the city to work and live. In just fifteen years, Cleveland's population had grown from 17,000 to more than 43,000, and the county's population had grown from 50,000 to 178,000. Trade unions had begun to receive charters to bring Cleveland's workers better pay and better working conditions, and a host of civic support mechanisms were created for a grown-up city and its citizens. These included hospitals, colleges, train stations, transportation systems, police departments, mail delivery to homes, a public library, formal cemeteries and amateur baseball clubs.

Abraham Lincoln had stopped in Cleveland in 1861 to deliver a speech on his trip from Springfield, Illinois, to his inauguration in Washington, D.C. Just four years later, his funeral train stopped in Cleveland, and his body lay in state at Public Square on its way back to Springfield after he was assassinated in Washington in the last month of the war. Cleveland took time and effort to assess where it had come from and where it had come. The Western Reserve Historical Society was formed, and the first history of Cleveland was published by Charles Whittlesey. Cleveland's industrial plant also expanded with the production of Bessemer Steel and the establishment in Cleveland of the Standard Oil Company and the Sherwin-Williams Company.

The establishment of these industries and others led to a more than doubling of Cleveland's population in just five years from 43,000 to 93,000. By 1870, this sudden population increase had made Cleveland the fifteenth-largest city in America. Cleveland's newfound success was coupled with an increase of the importance of the railroad's position in the city's structure. Because of the city's prominence, the Brotherhood of Locomotive Engineers relocated to the city, and in the 1870s, general railroad strikes threatened to alter the complexion of the railroad industry, leading to the creation of the Cleveland branch of the socialist labor party. By the end of the 1870s, Cleveland had become a city with a population of more than 160,000, and because the major-league city rated a professional baseball team, its amateur team joined the National League.

After the Civil War, political power shifted from the Democratic Party to the Republican Party. The primary driver of this change was an industrialist named Mark Hanna. Hanna had been elected to the Cleveland Board of Education in the late 1860s and had risen to the non-elected position of a powerful political boss. Hanna's power position was eventually challenged by fellow Republican Robert McKisson, who was elected mayor of Cleveland in 1895 on his promise to construct a modern water and sewer system. As well as becoming mayor, McKisson also took Hanna's political boss position and built a political machine that took control of the local Republican Party. Like all good political bosses, McKisson directed public money to his political friends. In a throwback to its Civil War days, when Cleveland's political parties had come together to support Lincoln and the war effort, McKisson was defeated after serving two terms by cooperation between the Democrats and Hanna-backed Republicans. By the end of the 1880s, Cleveland's population had grown to more than 260,000, and it was the nation's tenth-largest city. In 1888, the city also looked back

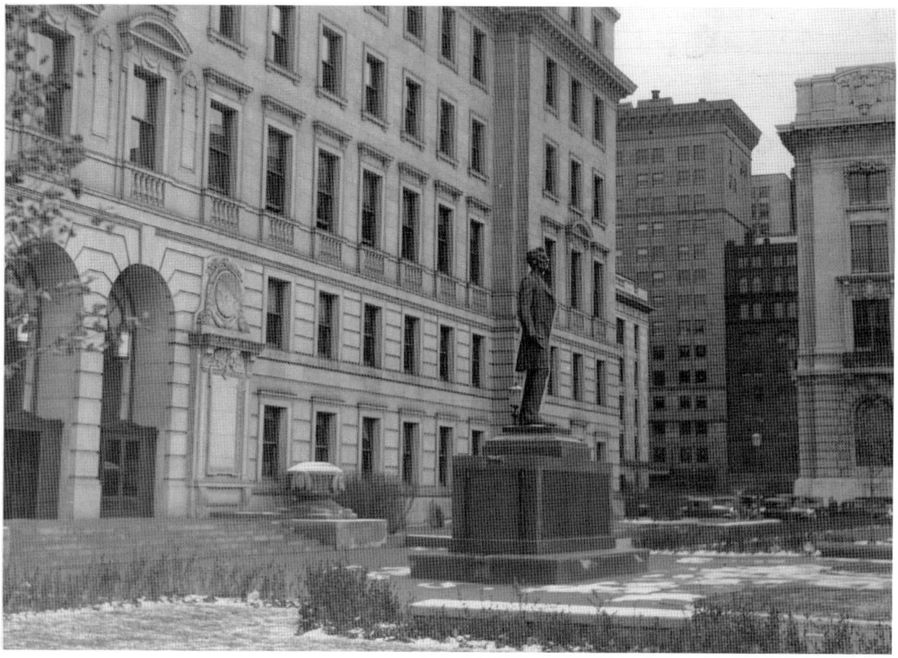

Statue of Abraham Lincoln outside the Mall-side entrance of the Cleveland Board of Education, one of the Group Plan buildings on the Mall's eastern edge. *Cleveland Memory Project.*

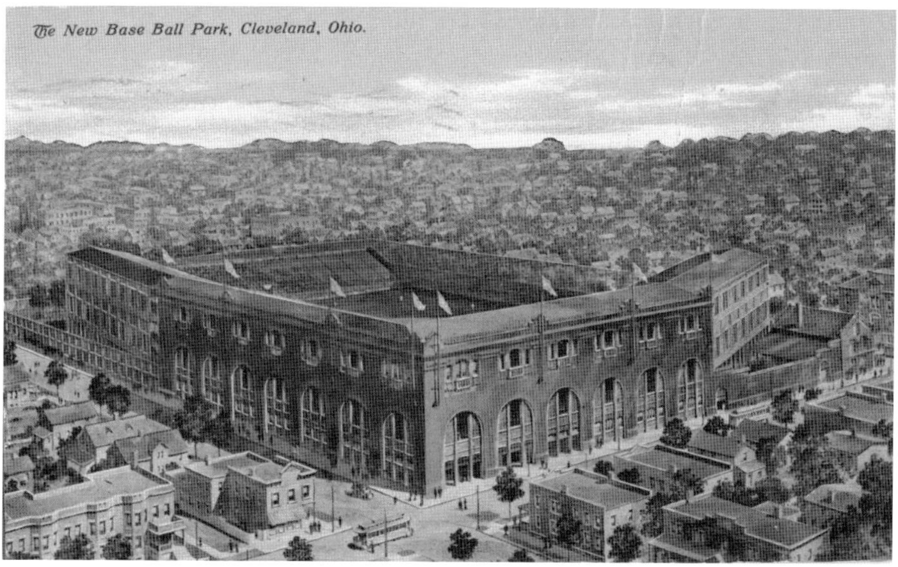

The reconstructed National League Park in Cleveland, Ohio, in 1910. League Park was the original home field of the Cleveland Spiders and then the Cleveland Indians baseball teams. *Cleveland Memory Project.*

on its origins, and a seated statue of Moses Cleaveland was dedicated on Public Square.

The 1890s in Cleveland were a time of a continued push toward respect and modernization. The Central Viaduct high-level bridge was built in the late 1880s to link Cleveland's east and west sides and connect its downtown with its southern neighbors across the Cuyahoga River. The idea for a new bridge had been introduced ten years earlier, but it was met with initial opposition; the resolution for the expenditure of $1 million for its construction wasn't approved by the city council until 1883. Because of the many valleys and gorges that had been formed by its glacial origins, Cleveland became a city of bridges. The bridge's main section was 2,839 feet long, and its second section included a swing section over the river to allow taller ships to pass under it. This section was replaced in 1912 with a stationary overhead truss bridge, which was 100 feet above the river. The decision to replace the swing bridge was triggered by the loss of a streetcar and seventeen of its passengers when a safety switch failed while the swinging section was open. The main portion of the bridge was closed in 1941 when it was determined to be unsafe, and its scrap iron was used in World War II.

INDUSTRY MEETS TECHNOLOGY

Technology also took a giant leap in Cleveland in the 1890s with the installation of a Brush arc light on Public Square, the establishment of the Cleveland Telephone Company and the Cleveland School of Art, the formation of the Case School of Applied Sciences, the relocation of Western Reserve College to Cleveland (the Case School and Western Reserve College would later merge to become Case Western Reserve University) and the formation of the Civil Engineers Club (later to become the Cleveland Engineering Society).

Cleveland's famous Euclid Beach opened in 1894 and operated for seventy-five years at a location on the Lake Erie shoreline at East 156th Street and Nottingham Road, about eight miles east of downtown Cleveland. The park was incorporated by a group of Cleveland investors and was patterned after New York's Coney Island. The Dudley S. Humphrey family took over management of the park in 1901 and changed it into a family-oriented park. Nearly forty years later, Humphrey would become one of the organizers and financers of Cleveland's Great Lakes Exposition. The park's archway entrance, which was declared a historic Cleveland landmark in 1973, is the only feature that remains of the park. Many efforts were made in the 1890s to connect Cleveland with its suburbs, including the first interurban service between Cleveland and Akron and Bedford, Ohio.

Just before the turn of the century, Cleveland's professional baseball team, the Cleveland Spiders, won baseball's Temple Cup. And in 1897, the Winton Bicycle Company responded to the rise of the popularity of the automobile and became the Winton Motor Carriage Company, an early pioneer in the manufacturing of automobiles. In the year 1900, Cleveland's automobile production companies spurred the establishment of the Cleveland Automobile Club. In part of its pioneering efforts to popularize the automobile, owner Alexander Winton drove one of his automobiles from Cleveland to New York. Winton's cars were high-end models, and his venture ceased production after a quarter century due to his company's inability to compete with automobile manufacturers that were producing more affordable automobiles.

CLEVELAND MOVES INTO THE TWENTIETH CENTURY

At the start of the new century, the 1900 census reported that Cleveland's population had risen to 382,000, making it the nation's seventh-largest city. Cuyahoga County's population had also risen to 439,000. The first White Corporation steam car was produced in 1900, and in 1901, the Cleveland Blues, which were the forerunners of the Cleveland Indians, were established as a new team in baseball's American League. Also in that year, Cleveland's most popular mayor to date, Tom Johnson, was elected.

Cleveland gained some unwanted attention when a Northern Ohio resident, Leon Czolgosz, an American anarchist and former steel worker, assassinated President William McKinley in Buffalo, New York, in September 1901. Czolgosz was executed just over seven weeks later. At age seventeen, Czolgosz began working at the Cleveland Rolling Mill Company, where he took part in labor strikes. When the company closed for some time in 1893 to reduce costs, Czolgosz joined a series of socialist clubs that preached anarchy. In about 1900, Czolgosz heard speeches by political radical Emma Goldman, whom he quickly befriended. Radical newspapers of the time

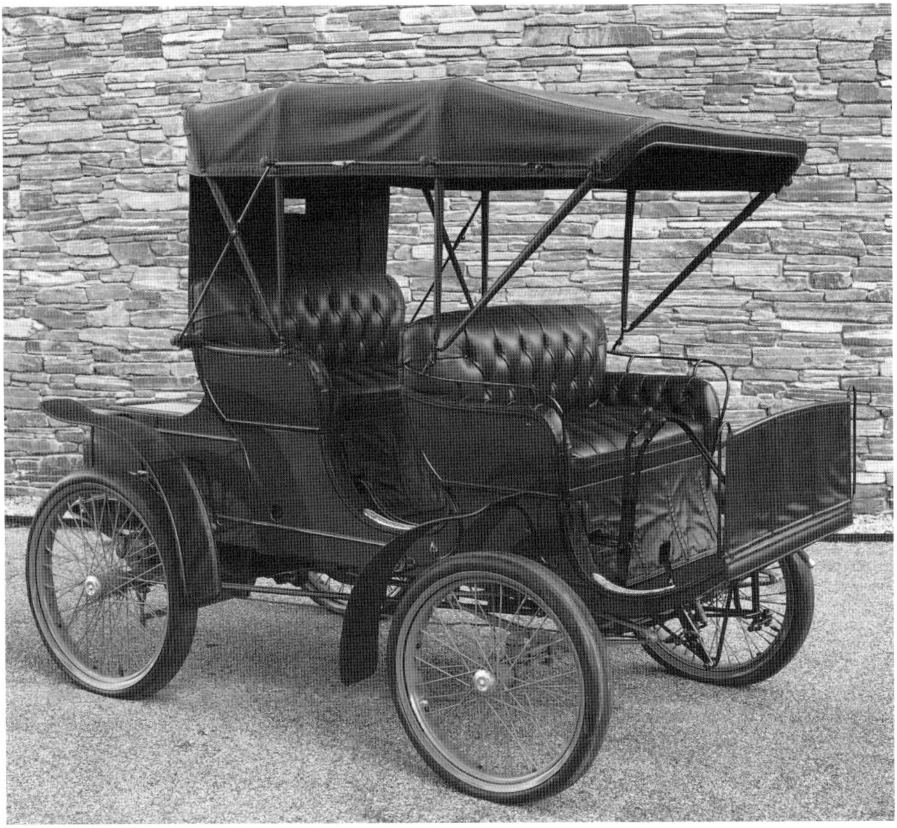

This 1899 model of a Winton Motor Car Company automobile is an example of Cleveland's extensive automobile manufacturing industry, which was active from the 1890s to the 1920s. *Case Western Reserve University.*

took note of his extreme, violent views and uncharacteristically printed public warnings about him.

Czolgosz quickly came to view the government as the cause of injustices to the common man and decided to take matters into his own hands. He made plans to shoot the president in a receiving line at the Temple of Music at the Pan American Exposition in Buffalo, New York. He fired twice at the president, who died eight days later of an abdominal infection. Czolgosz pleaded guilty to first-degree murder charges and was executed for his crime after refusing to be party to an insanity defense. In a strange turn, it was decided that sulfuric acid would be poured into his coffin to totally consume his body.

IMMIGRATION SHAPES CLEVELAND'S FUTURE

Cleveland's identity and its soul lie in its ethnic heritage. Throughout its history, Cleveland has been the epitome of a melting pot of people from all corners of the world. Most of Cleveland's colonial settlers had British roots. Even though one of the reasons that the Connecticut Land Company's venture capitalists traveled to the banks of the Cuyahoga River (the western extent of their allotted territory) was to lay a claim to the area before British or French interests could do the same, they were of British roots themselves. Cleveland's citizens have had a tradition of originating from a vast number of the world's countries. At one time, Cleveland was known to have the largest number of distinct urban ethnic enclaves.

This factor has given the city its central character as a collection of ethnic neighborhoods that provide the city with a never-ending variety of languages, foods, religions, music and cultural traditions. People from all ends of the earth have headed to the United States from the early 1800s to the present to seek better opportunities, to escape persecutions and to take advantage of the prosperity that the United States could provide. Many of these people were drawn to the Midwest's factories because they offered wealth through jobs. They brought with them their traditions and religions, which were and are central to their everyday lives.

Cleveland's Polish immigrants have long been its largest ethnic population. Polish immigrants began to arrive in Cleveland in the mid-nineteenth century to work in the city's steel mills and garment industry. Cleveland's Poles originally settled on the city's southeast side and, later, in the mid-twentieth century, and although many still live in those same neighborhoods, many of them migrated to Cleveland's immediate southern suburbs.

Cleveland's Irish settlers began arriving in the 1820s, drawn to the area to work on the construction of the Ohio and Erie Canal and on the construction of Cleveland's docks. Cleveland's earliest Irish immigrants created an urban enclave on Cleveland's Whiskey Island, and today, Cleveland's Irish Parish is located in a near-west neighborhood adjacent to Cleveland's Flats District.

Cleveland's Italian immigrants, who began arriving in the mid-1800s, originally settled in Cleveland's near-east neighborhoods. Because they brought with them a collection of skills, they were important players in Cleveland's early economic success. Today's Italian urban enclave is centered on Cleveland's near-east Little Italy neighborhood.

Many of Cleveland's early German immigrants had originally settled in eastern states and moved to northeast Ohio later on. Like the Poles and the

Irish, they were drawn to Cleveland by jobs associated with the construction of the Ohio and Erie Canal. Many of Cleveland's German citizens settled in what today is Cleveland's Tremont neighborhood, which is adjacent to the downtown area to the south. Later generations of German families, who were craftsmen, butchers and brewers, settled in Cleveland's west side neighborhoods.

During much of the twentieth century, Cleveland had the largest Slovenian community in the United States. People of Slovenian origin began arriving in Cleveland in the late nineteenth century, and many of them settled in Cleveland's Newburgh area, in Cleveland's east side neighborhoods along St. Clair Avenue and in Cleveland's Collinwood neighborhood. Cleveland's Slovenians have been known for their ethnic polka music and for their involvement in political affairs.

Cleveland's first Chinese residents arrived in the mid-nineteenth century and settled in a small Cantonese neighborhood adjacent to Public Square on Ontario Street, where they established a one-block-long Chinatown neighborhood that featured several Chinese restaurants, laundries and specialty stores. This neighborhood was purposefully emptied by local law enforcement authorities to make way for other development. As Cleveland's downtown grew and prospered, the city's Chinese population moved farther east and developed a new Chinese-dominated neighborhood nearer to Cleveland's collegiate district.

Other major ethnic populations that settled in Cleveland during its developmental years include the Czechs, who arrived in the late nineteenth century, and a large Ukrainian population, who started to arrive in the Cleveland area in the mid-1870s and were followed later by Ukrainians who were seeking stability following the fall of the Soviet Union. In the 1870s, large numbers of Hungarians immigrated to the Cleveland area to work in its factories and machine shops. Like the Ukrainians, many additional Hungarians arrived in Cleveland after their flight from Europe following World War II and the Hungarian Revolution. Cleveland's link to its African American population dates back to its original non–Native American settlers. Cleveland's first African American settler was George Peake, who arrived in Cleveland in 1809, thirteen years after Moses Cleaveland founded the city. Over the years, Cleveland's African American citizens arrived in two major waves from America's southern states, in the late nineteenth and early twentieth century and then between 1940 and 1960. Other ethnic groups that settled in Cleveland include the Koreans, the Croatians, the Greeks, the Lithuanians and the Arab Americans.

By 1909, the city's population was more than 560,000, and it was now the nation's sixth-largest city. In 1910, the Group Plan's first structure, a new Federal Building, opened. Between 1910 and 1929, many of the villages that surrounded Cleveland were annexed. As well as continuing to annex existing villages by providing water and electric utility service throughout the Cuyahoga Valley region, a large number of new cities were incorporated through the 1950s. In 1912, the Cleveland City Club and the Junior League were established. The City Club of Cleveland is "Cleveland's Citadel of Free Speech" and provides a place for members to engage in social, political and economic discussions. The proceedings of its weekly debates are recorded and distributed for broadcast in hundreds of cities nationwide. Cleveland's Junior League is a women's group that promotes voluntarism, develops the potential of women and improves the community through effective volunteer activities and leadership.

POLITICS BECOMES IMPORTANT IN THE CITY

Cleveland's government structure underwent another change in 1912 when the city's voters adopted a home rule charter. The charter removed state-imposed restrictions of the management of its city that had limited the city's ability to effectively respond to problems arising from its rapid growth during the nineteenth and early twentieth centuries. Early in the twentieth century, Cleveland was home to pioneer carmakers, including steam car builders White and Gaeth and electric car company Baker. After a succession of ineffective Democrat-led government administrations and a series of corrupt Republican-led administrations, Clevelanders voted for change and elected Democrat Tom L. Johnson into the mayor's office in 1901. Johnson led reform movements that eventually brought a home rule form of government to Cleveland, and he was the principal motivator behind Cleveland taking on the challenge of engineering and promoting the development of Daniel Burnham's 1903 Group Plan to bring order to and develop Cleveland's central civic and business core. With cabinet members Newton D. Baker and Harris R. Cooley, Johnson brought order and respect to Cleveland's city government.

After being elected Cleveland's mayor in 1911, Baker sought more freedom for the city from state-imposed restrictions on municipal management. Baker pushed for home rule and helped write the 1912 Ohio constitutional amendment giving municipalities the right to govern themselves. By campaigning for its passage in 1913, Baker became influential in selecting the commission to write Cleveland's first home rule charter. In 1916, Baker declined to run for a third term and instead returned to private practice of law. Baker was succeeded as mayor by Harry L. Davis.

In 1914, the Cleveland Foundation was established under the trusteeship of the Cleveland Trust Company (now AmeriTrust). The foundation is a philanthropic institution that funds worthy causes in Cuyahoga, Lake and Geauga Counties. Over the years, these investments have included the Great Lakes Exposition, the Cleveland Commission on Higher Education and cultural institutions such as the Cleveland Orchestra, the Cleveland Museum of Art and the Cleveland Opera. In the same year, Cleveland was chosen to be the location of the Fourth District headquarters of the Federal Reserve Bank.

Toward a More Beautiful City

The years of 1916 and 1917 were active years in Cleveland. In those years, the first production by the Cleveland Play House was staged, the Cleveland Museum of Art opened to the public, the Cleveland Orchestra gave its first performance, the Women's City Club was established, Cleveland's new city hall was dedicated, the Detroit-Superior High Level Bridge was opened to traffic and the Cleveland Metroparks system was organized. The Cleveland Metroparks system is a collection of twelve park reservations in Cuyahoga and Medina Counties. In 1975, the district acquired control of the Cleveland Zoo. The chain of twelve reservations that surround the metropolitan are referred to as the "Emerald Necklace." Cleveland's park district was the idea of William Stinchcomb. His organizational efforts secured the passage of state legislation that permitted the establishment of park districts and the creation of Cleveland's park district.

Stinchcomb was appointed director of the district in 1921 and served in that position until 1957. In its early years, the district's efforts were centered on the acquisition of suitable properties to be maintained in a natural state. Today, the district includes nature interpretive centers, bridle and hiking trails, a linked system of park drives, picnic areas and shelter houses, wildlife management areas, swimming beaches and public golf courses. By 1920, Cleveland had grown to be the nation's fifth-largest city with a population of 797,000, and the county's population had reached almost 1 million. An important vote was also held that year that approved the move of the city's main railroad terminal from the lakefront to a new set of buildings adjacent to Public Square. Finally, an important civic event occurred in 1920 when the Cleveland Indians defeated the Brooklyn Robins in the 1920 baseball World Series.

Over a century of time, Cleveland rose from a mostly deserted, swampy area at the non-distinct mouth of the Cuyahoga River Valley to become one of the largest cities in the United States. It had survived the challenges of rapid change and questionable government and had established itself as an important industrial center and a hub for the transport of America's natural resources. At the turn of the twentieth century, Cleveland faced an uncertain future that had become typical of America's industrial cities, but with new leadership, the city looked forward to a brighter future—one that might be developed under new mayor Tom Johnson according to the City Beautiful movement, an architecture and urban planning philosophy that had been championed at the 1893 Columbian World Exposition in Chicago and that had shown great promise for reforming and restructuring aging industrial cities by bringing importance to city beautification and order.

Cleveland, along with Chicago, Detroit and Washington, D.C., adopted the City Beautiful movement's new urban planning philosophy in the hope of creating new cities that were based on moral and civic virtue as well as social order. The nation's industrial cities had been overcome by overcrowding, poor living conditions, rampant crime, poverty and issues associated with the challenge of assimilating dissimilar populations. The movement's philosophy wasn't perfect, and its success depended on how and who implemented it. The city's efforts also faced many challenges brought about by changing times and worldwide struggles, but Cleveland succeeded to a point in bringing about change that eventually helped it survive and prosper through the tough times ahead.

A City Beautiful

The City Beautiful Movement

Divine Nature gave the fields, human art built the cities.
—*Marcus Terentius Varro,* De Re Rustica

The City Beautiful movement was a city planning and design concept that started in the United States as a response to overcrowding in urban tenements and poor urban living conditions. The overcrowding was a direct side effect of the rapid urban population increases that were seen in the second half of the 1800s and the first quarter of the 1900s due to record immigration to the United States from all corners of the world, higher birth rates and internal migration of rural populations to America's large industrial cities. There were serious problems in U.S. cities before World War I. Most political, civic and business leaders in America's cities during the late 1800s and early 1900s focused their energies on building their industrial plants and the infrastructure that supported them and had ignored serious problems that were an unfortunate coupling to rapid growth: poverty, disease, social unrest, discrimination and the exclusion of portions of the population in achieving personal success.

Chicago hosted the World's Columbian Exposition in 1893, an event that was seen as the first large-scale implementation of the art-centered design ethic that was championed by proponents of the City Beautiful movement. Thirteen years later, in 1906, American journalist Upton Sinclair's 1906 novel *The Jungle* alerted America's industrial cities, and the city of Chicago, that the substandard working and living conditions of exploited workers and immigrants had not improved. The implementation of the City Beautiful movement was first championed in the United States by Chicago architect Daniel Burnham, who, along with a hand-chosen group of architects from eastern states and artists such as famed sculptor Augustus Saint-Gaudens, sought to use their urban planning and design talents to transform America's injured cities. In 1893, Burnham and his design associates used the Columbian Exposition to showcase their ideas of the application of a monumental architectural style, uniform building scale and the use of art and sculpture and classical design motifs drawn from Europe's cities to transform America's cities. Burnham's group's design work at the Columbian Exposition resulted in the construction of a model city in grand scale known as the "White City."

Critics of the time criticized the movement's aims for not addressing America's real urban problems and instead focusing on superficial design elements. The wide streets, monumental buildings, beautiful fountains and lagoons that were featured in the movement's plans were an unrealistic reflection of America's urban problems and did nothing to address real urban troubles of poverty, poor sanitation and ineffective transportation systems. Burnham's White City plans looked good, but his urban design solutions turned their back on these problems and, in some ways, exacerbated problems by displacing people from their urban neighborhoods to make room for grandiose structures.

Chicago's exposition was a popular show, though, and out of desperation, many people accepted that it might be possible that reforming their cities in the style of the City Beautiful movement could enable their cities to continue to grow and thrive and, at the same time, wash away substandard conditions in their urban neighborhoods. Even though there was no evidence that the movement's design ethic would result in positive change, it dominated urban development thought in America and in many foreign countries for decades. The influence of the movement's perceived successes in the early years of the twentieth century had a lasting influence on later housing and urban design projects that were conceived decades later.

Similar City Beautiful movement–inspired urban planning efforts were conceived around the world. In Britain, the "Garden City" movement dominated urban renewal in London's suburbs. After a while, the two movements became interchangeable, with City Beautiful design ideas of

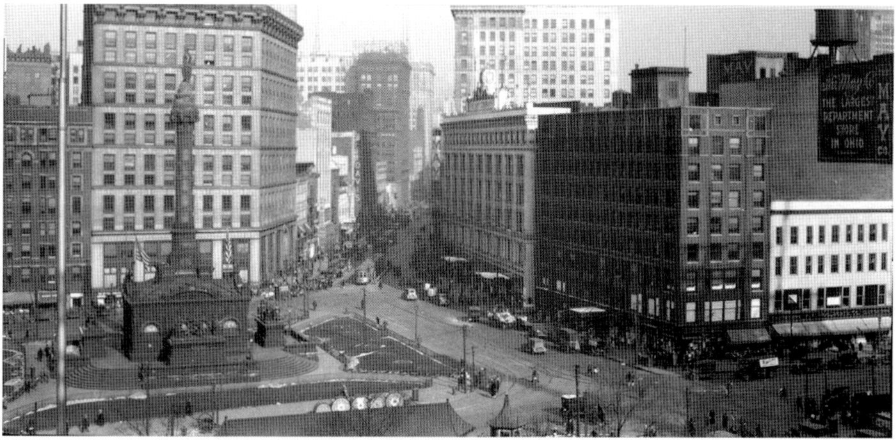

This early 1930s view across Cleveland's Public Square looks east down Euclid Avenue. At the time, the May Company was Ohio's largest department store. *Schwartz.*

the use of the monumental Beaux-Arts architectural style being used in European cities and Garden City design ideas of using rural elements in urban design influencing the development of some of America's "new cities."

Based on Burnham's success in marketing City Beautiful movement's design elements, they were readily adopted by other architects and urban planners. French American architect Louis Masqueray employed the movement's design style that was used so successfully in Chicago for his design for the Louisiana Purchase Exposition in St. Louis in 1904, as well as the movement's use of the Beaux-Arts architectural style in his later design of a cathedral in St. Paul, Minnesota.

One of the first examples of the use of City Beautiful movement design principles was in an important plan for the redesign of Washington, D.C.'s monumental core, including the creation of the Mall. The 1901 plan's intent was to fulfill elements of Pierre Charles L'Enfant's plan for Washington that weren't fully realized after the building of the Capitol City had begun one hundred years earlier. In addition to Daniel Burnham, the design team for the Washington, D.C., plan included the future father of landscape architecture, Frederick Law Olmsted; sculptor Augustus Saint-Gaudens; and other architects and city planners. Basing their design elements on buildings and spaces they had observed in Europe, the planning team hoped to make changes in Washington that would eliminate the city's drab and dusty nature and change it into a green oasis.

The primary elements of the Washington plan included the addition of large, formal green spaces—using Olmsted's concept of urban "re-creation" spaces, like those he would later create in Boston and New York—and employing the concept of creating order by removing urban slums and substandard housing and replacing them with orderly rectilinear open spaces surrounded and enclosed by Neoclassical buildings of uniform height and scale. In addition to the plan that would become Washington's Great Mall, the plan included the construction of grand temple-like memorials and the Burnham-designed Union Station. Burnham recognized that the railroad was king, and most of his plans included the construction of a grand train station.

Because of the scale and complexity of City Beautiful–inspired plans—public acceptance of design concepts, acquisition of property, assembly of project funding, demolition of existing structures, relocation of displaced populations and multi-year construction plans—many of these complex plans were interrupted over time by uncontrollable events that happened in the real world that was revolving around them. Washington's plan was no exception, as the completion of the plan was interrupted by World War I. Following the end of the war in 1918, work on the construction of the Lincoln Memorial, which was one of the plan's important design elements, was resumed and completed in 1922. In the end, Burnham's Washington, D.C., plan took a generation to complete.

Being awarded the contract for the Washington design was a business coup for Burnham and the architects and artists who would assist him in his future projects. The success and visibility of the Washington plan proved to be influential in Burnham being awarded urban beautification projects in many other cities, including Chicago, Illinois; Baltimore, Maryland; Cleveland and Columbus, Ohio; Detroit, Michigan; New York City; Philadelphia, Pennsylvania; and many other cities from Seattle, Washington, to Coral Gables, Florida. Burnham's use of interchangeable teams of landscape architects, city planners, artists and sculptors enabled him to effectively respond to the varying design challenges that projects required.

Implementation of City Beautiful–inspired urban planning and design wasn't without its problems, however. In addition to the unsureness of whether a plan would ever be fully realized, these ideas were often criticized as being superficial plans that didn't include measures that directly improved the living conditions in a city's urban neighborhoods.

THE BURNHAM DESIGN GROUP

Daniel Burnham was born in Henderson, New York, and moved to Chicago, Illinois, at the age of eight. After completing his primary education, Burnham applied to Harvard and Yale but was rejected for admission to both universities. He then tried politics but failed at that. Finally, he apprenticed as a draftsman under William Jenny. Burnham's decision to apprentice under Jenny was probably the best he ever made. After graduating college in 1856, he served as an engineer in the Civil War. After the war, Jenny returned to Chicago and opened an architectural firm that specialized in designing and building commercial buildings and in urban planning. Jenny was a college classmate of Gustave Eiffel, the designer of Paris's Eiffel Tower, and is credited with championing new construction methods that allowed him to design and build the world's first skyscraper in 1884, the ten-story Home Insurance Building. These new construction techniques allowed buildings to be built that weighed only one-third as much as buildings that were built using a standard masonry structure. Jenny's use of metal girders and struts enabled him to build taller buildings, changing the face of every city in the world.

In the late nineteenth century, Jenny was mentor to many who would become the most influential architects of the early 1900s, including Louis Sullivan, Daniel Burnham, William Holabird and Martin Roche. In the 1870s, Burnham joined with John Root in founding their own architectural firm that specialized in designing and building residential and commercial buildings. Burnham and Root's successful firm was at times criticized for building unnecessarily lavish, extravagant structures. The firm's greatest achievement was a commission to coordinate the construction of the 1893 Columbian Exposition. During their partnership, Burnham, who was a handsome and engaging person, took on the role of a talented designer and salesperson who could sell projects to clients, while Root was the firm's creative genius. After Root's death in 1891, Burnham took on the work of completing the coordination and planning for the Columbian Exposition. In that role, Burnham worked with many of the nation's leading architects, and in taking a lead role in the exposition's success, he became the nation's most influential architect.

Following the exposition's six-month run in 1893, Daniel Burnham and Company took on a city planning project for the City of Chicago, which became the foundation of the City Beautiful movement. The firm's Chicago plan, which was the first to lay out a plan for a total redesign of an American city, incorporated artistic elements into its design and stressed that every citizen should be within walking distance of a park. While having a lasting influence on Chicago's future development, only parts of the firm's far-reaching plans were ever implemented—a trend that would be repeated in most of Burnham's future urban planning projects. These projects included plans for Washington, D.C., in 1901, Cleveland in 1903 and San Francisco in 1905. Burnham is famous for saying, "Make no little plans. They have no magic to stir men's blood and probably will not themselves be realized." Burnham's quote sums up his work. Nonetheless, Burnham was often criticized for making plans that were too large, and many of his plans were indeed never fully realized.

CLEVELAND'S GROUP PLAN

Cleveland's manifestation of the City Beautiful movement was seen in the "Group Plan." The plan was a design solution that was devised by an architecture and planning firm that was fronted by famed architects and planners Daniel Burnham, John M. Carrère and Arnold R. Brunner in response to Cleveland's Group Plan Commission's call for a "civic center" between Cleveland's New England–inspired Public Square and its lakefront. The Burnham group's 1903 plan was proposed to be a classic representation of City Beautiful thought—a modern, artificially lit grouping of Neoclassical civic buildings of uniform scale in height and mass, embracing an open civic area filled with grand fountains, sculptures and European-inspired, formally planted areas indicative of the grounds of Versailles. The Burnham group's design solution was reflective of designs from the Columbian Exposition from ten years earlier.

It was going to be a hard sell for Cleveland's civic leaders to convince the city's citizens that the project was going to be worth supporting when city planners from across the country were criticizing the plan as being impractical and unlikely to even address, let alone solve, Cleveland's real needs of relieving poverty and removing squalor from the city's neighborhoods. Urban planner Jens Jensen labeled Cleveland's Group Plan and other City Beautiful–inspired plans as "grandiose, inhumane, imperialistic and undemocratic."

It was apparent to everyone in Cleveland that the collection of run-down shacks, bars, houses of ill repute and slum housing that dominated Cleveland's downtown core needed a solution, but would Burnham's plan

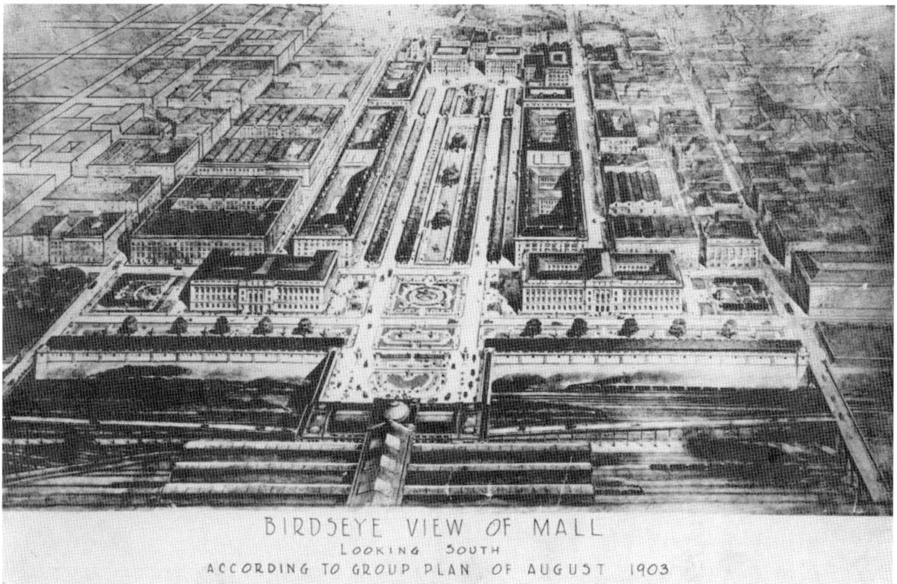

Daniel Burnham's conceptual sketch of the 1903 Group Plan for Cleveland, Ohio. This view looks to the south, across Cleveland's proposed Great Mall. *Cleveland Memory Project.*

solve these problems or just shove the problems farther east down Cleveland's main streets; maybe more importantly, would it ever be possible for the plan to be realized, and would it solve Cleveland's lakefront problem?

Cleveland's "lakefront problem" revolved around the common thought that there was a need to consolidate the city's railroad connections into a "Union Terminal" that in Burnham's plan was represented by a palatial Union Station, located where the majority of Cleveland's rail lines were located—on the lakefront—at the northern terminus of a "Grand Mall." In Burnham's plan, the Union Station would serve the same purpose as the Lincoln Memorial served in the Washington plan: a temple to celebrate an important idea and ethic. The project was an expensive undertaking. By the end of World War I, more than $25 million in tax money would be spent on it, and more funding would be needed in the future to finish the job. Cleveland's mayor, Tom Johnson, loved the idea, and in the end, he was able to sell it to Cleveland's voters as a project that would improve the city's image and draw business, industries, employment and prosperity to the city. Selling the project was made easier by the fact that most of Cleveland's voters didn't live in the downtown slums that would be displaced by the project.

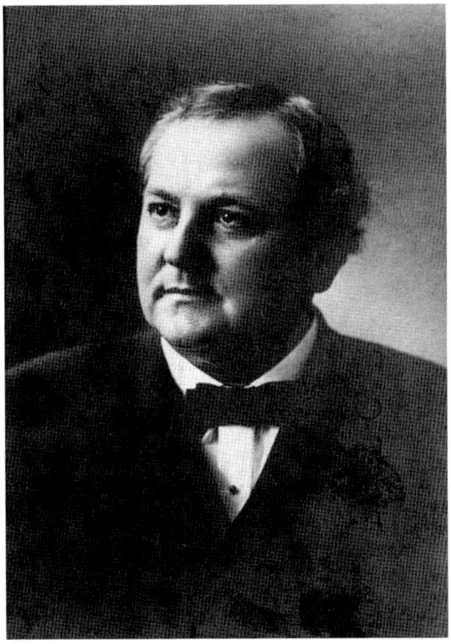

Postcard photograph image of Tom L. Johnson, who was elected mayor of Cleveland, Ohio, in 1901 and then elected for three additional terms. *Cleveland Memory Project.*

In his sales pitch, Mayor Johnson stressed that after the project was completed, visitors to the city would enter it by disembarking their trains in a palatial terminal and then climb the lakefront bluffs via grand staircases and ramps that would open onto a beautiful public garden space, surrounded by Neoclassical buildings that would give them the feeling that they were in an important, vibrant and successful city. A hitch in the mayor's vision was that the railroads weren't keen on funding their share of the project because they didn't think that it would be a benefit to their freight traffic business, the profits from which far outweighed profits from passenger traffic. They decided they would be happier if improvements were made to the existing 1864-vintage train station that was just outside downtown, whereby their profits would be kept safe. In the end, through financial and political twists and turns, the old train station was demolished, the idea of a palatial lakefront train station was abandoned and the city's new Union Station was located beneath a new "Terminal Tower"—a building that when completed would be the third-tallest building in the world.

THE GROUP PLAN MEETS ITS TERMINAL CHALLENGE

The Terminal Tower project would for years cripple the chance of Cleveland's Group Plan being a success. The tower project grew out of a desire by two eccentric Cleveland brothers, Oris and Mantis Van Sweringen, to improve the chances of their plans to develop a suburban housing development east of Cleveland. The brothers decided that further development of their Shaker Heights project was being held back by a lack of an efficient means of moving people to and from the Shaker Heights housing development and downtown Cleveland. By 1909, the brothers had bought land near Public Square to facilitate the development of a terminus for their transit line between Shaker Heights and downtown Cleveland, but their plans steadily expanded. By the mid-1920s, they had made plans for a "super transit" system that would serve the whole of Cuyahoga County, and in a few more years, their plans attracted additional investors who proposed the development of commuter and passenger railroad lines that would stretch the sixty miles between Painesville and Lorain, Ohio.

The brothers and their fellow investors started to think even bigger, and they realized that there was an opportunity for the development adjacent to Public Square for a Union Station that would be large enough to accommodate the concentration of the myriad commuter transit lines that were being proposed along the Lake Erie shoreline. It was decided that the best thing to do would be to take advantage of an opportunity to concentrate hotels, office space, retail space, warehouses, freight offloading stations and rail connections between the lakeshore rail lines into as tight a space as possible to provide amenities to commuters. So, between 1917 and 1918, the Terminal Tower project was born and was codified and financially supported by a public referendum to develop a railway station in the Terminal Tower location and abandon the idea of a Union Terminal at the apex of Burnham's Great Mall. By the late 1920s, the Terminal Tower project had been completed, and Cleveland's Union Station would be located beneath the fifty-two-story Terminal Tower—a civic monument to the plans and schemes of two brothers.

The Terminal Tower fronts Public Square diagonally and looks out over the square toward the Mall and its surrounding civic buildings. This placement was purposely done to visually link the two projects, but because the tower project drew attention away from the Mall—and because the city's financial resources had been tapped by the now-expansive tower-area project—the city's enthusiasm for development of the Mall had waned. It would have been impossible to know in 1930, when the Terminal Tower was dedicated, that the need for the space that was dedicated to its commuter rail lines, ticket booths and associated mechanisms would be short-lived because of the rise of the automobile. It's interesting to note that the nation's canal system, the construction of which began around 1820, had seen a similar fate when it was outmoded by the railroad only forty years later in 1860. The heyday of America's passenger railroads lasted twice as long, from 1880 to 1940, but the size of the economic investment in the country's railroads was vastly larger.

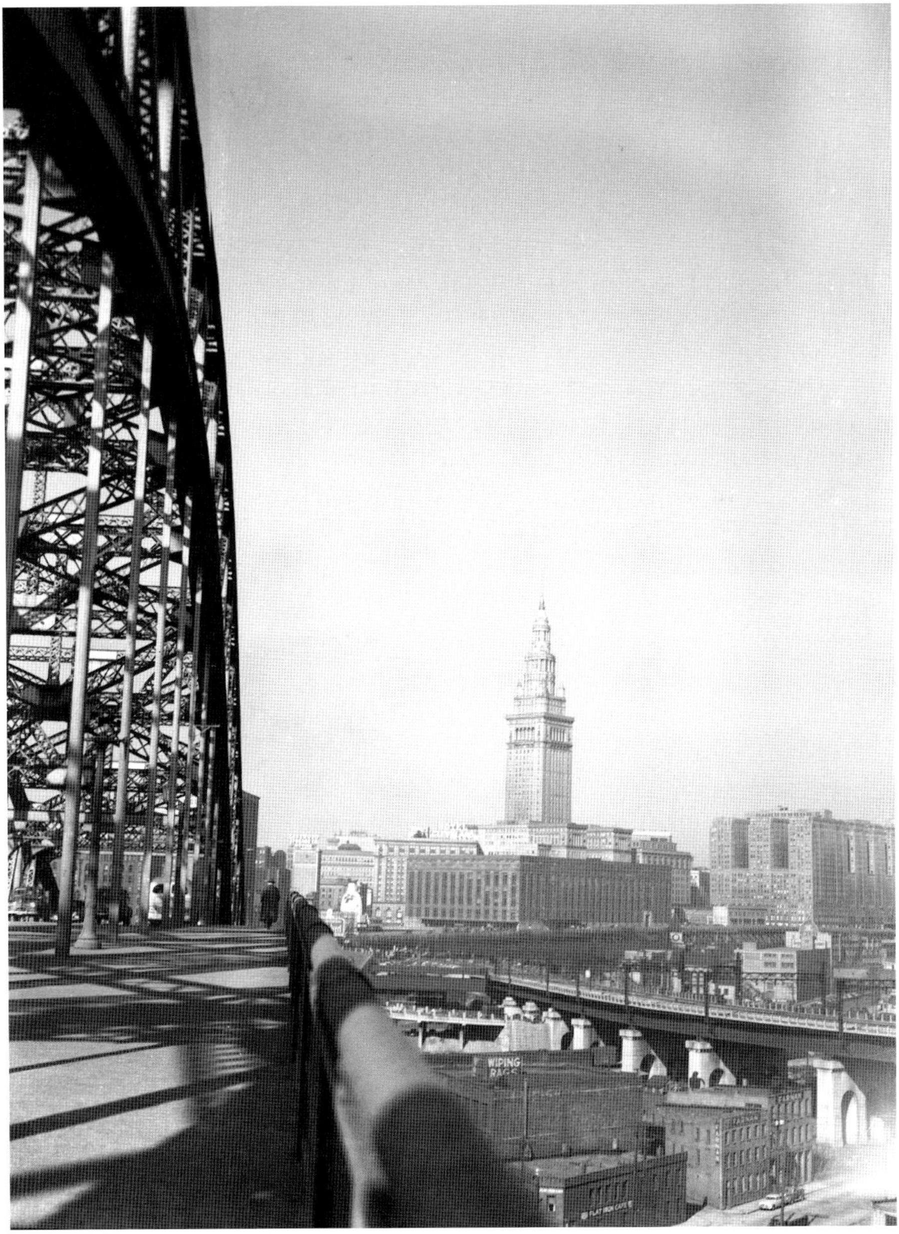

Circa 1940 view of the Terminal Tower, looking to the east from the edge of the Detroit-Superior Bridge over the Cuyahoga River and the industrial flats. *Schwartz*.

After completing a number of the Group Plan's elements, development of Cleveland's Great Mall and the area that surrounded it slacked off in the second and third decades of the twentieth century. One of the main drivers of the Group Plan's design was the vision and promise of a monumental terminus that would cap the design, in this case a grand Union Terminal along Cleveland's lakefront that would celebrate and honor the modernity and wealth that the railroads brought to the city and would acknowledge that the railroads were the king of commerce. The project's originators couldn't foresee, though, that the railroads weren't going to cooperate with the plan and that they would be more interested in maximizing their profits than they would be interested in playing their part in funding civic monuments. Nevertheless, plans had been made for a five-hundred-foot-wide three-part Great Mall surrounded by Neoclassical buildings that would house the city's seats of government, education and law. The development of these elements limped on through the challenge of addressing the railroads and the trial of World War I.

The Group Plan Limps Forward

Burnham's Group Plan design had been lauded by some as being, on paper, the best embodiment to date of the City Beautiful movement's ideals. Cleveland made a good start in carrying out the construction of major elements of the plan. Construction of Cleveland's Federal Building was completed in 1910, and the construction of the new Cuyahoga County Courthouse and its twin along Lakeside Avenue (Cleveland City Hall) were completed in 1911 and 1916, respectively. Additionally, three buildings that were intended to enclose the eastern and southern edges of the Mall were also completed: the Public Auditorium, which was completed in 1922; Cleveland's Main Public Library building, which was completed in 1925; and the Board of Education Building, which was completed in 1930. Development of the two primary buildings that were meant to enclose the remaining western edge of the Mall was never started, and the central mall area remained a large rubble-strewn field.

Development of the Group Plan's central mall lagged far behind development and construction of the civic buildings meant to surround it. The three-part Mall area sat vacant for many years, and with the exception of its brief vital moment when it took center stage during the Great Lakes

Exposition in the mid-1930s, further development of the Mall area waited until the 1950s and 1960s, when a set of pared-down fountains and statuary was installed. The Burnham group's original plans for the Mall area included gardens, fountains, formal strolling areas, open spaces for public gatherings (inspired by formal spaces that he had seen in European cities) and classically inspired sculptures and other artworks that would signal to people that Cleveland was an important place. While Cleveland's initial plan for a City Beautiful movement–inspired masterpiece reflected the best of what could be expected, it also embodied the worst of what critics of City Beautiful plans predicted—that these plans were too grandiose and too expensive to ever have a chance of being completed according to plan if they depended on public funding.

A major push to complete the development of the Mall and the remaining buildings that would enclose its western edge was made in the mid-1920s and received the support of a small group of investors that held out hope that the Group Plan's original intents could still be realized. To get a better picture of the status of the remaining area within the Group Plan's

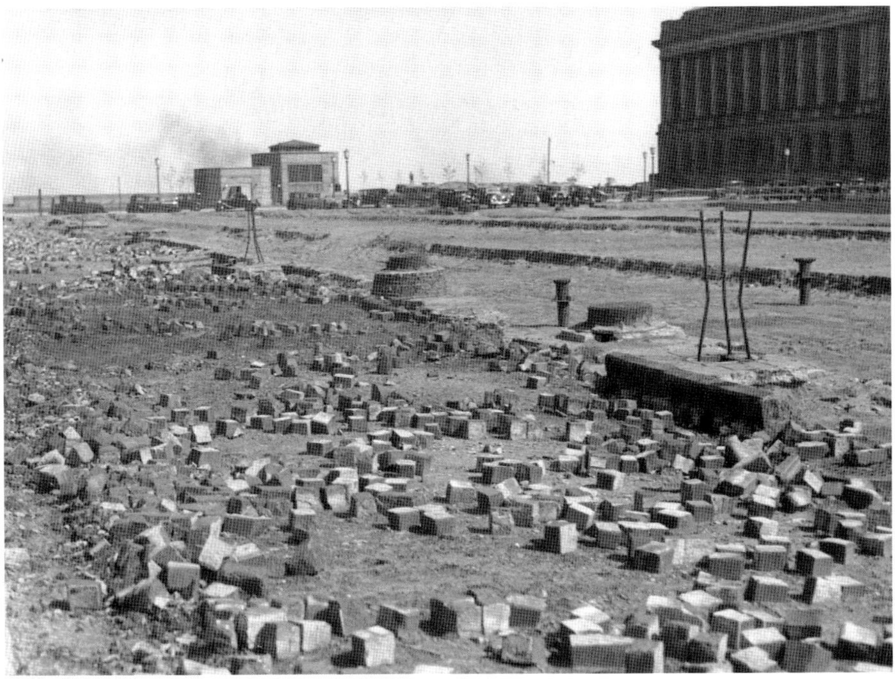

This 1932 photograph looks north toward Lake Erie, over a then vacant area that was proposed to be Cleveland's Great Mall. Cleveland's newly constructed Public Hall and city hall can be seen in the upper-right corner. *Cleveland Memory Project.*

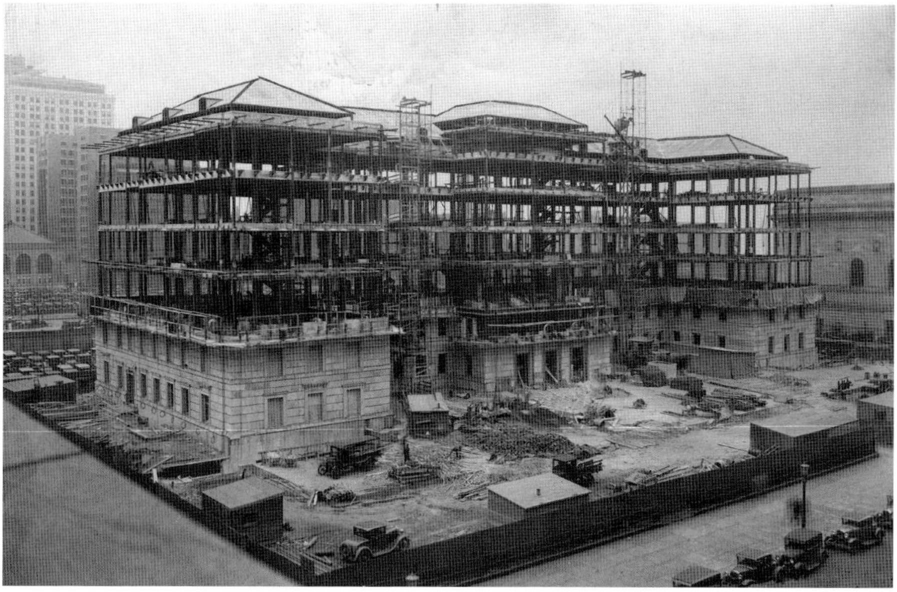

One of the Group Plan buildings, the Cleveland Board of Education Building, under construction in 1930 on the eastern edge of Cleveland's Great Mall. *Cleveland Memory Project.*

footprint that still need to be developed, a parcel-by-parcel photographic survey was commissioned. Some of the images that resulted from that project have been included in this book and are being seen for the first time since they were produced ninety years ago. A small number of images from that set and from another set of images that were produced in the 1930s were included in a book, *1936–1937 Great Lakes Exposition*, written by Brad Schwartz (one of the co-authors of this book) and published in 2016 by Arcadia Publishing.

Cleveland was facing other challenges brought about by the economic conditions that its citizens and workforce were experiencing. After World War I, Cleveland and other major industrial cities were faced with uprisings and protests by workers in response to working conditions that was inspired and backed by socialist groups. Many of Cleveland's out-of-work men were living on the street and in abandoned areas adjacent to railroad frontages along the city's lakefront. Cleveland and other cities weathered these challenges and continued to grow. By 1920, Cleveland's population had grown to a point where the city was the nation's fifth-largest city.

Advancement in the Arts and Sciences

In the first quarter of the twentieth century, Cleveland's industrial plant was prospering on the shoulders of its overworked citizens and around its less fortunate citizens. Industrial production had been sparked by World War I, and the city was finding its cultural footing thanks in large part to donations and endowments from its wealthiest citizens. The twenty years between the mid-1910s and mid-1930s in Cleveland proved to be an unprecedented time of advancements in the arts and sciences. The start of this period can be best marked by the opening of the Cleveland Museum of Art in 1916. The establishment of Cleveland's art museum was funded by initial donations by Hinman Hurlbut, John Huntington and Horace Kelley and was built on property that was donated by Jeptha Wade. Wade's land donation would become the center of Cleveland's University Circle, a collection of internationally respected museums, esteemed educational institutions and advanced medical facilities. These initial donations were backed up by donations from Cleveland's leading families, who contributed works of art to the museum. Over the years, the Cleveland Museum of Art has grown to be considered one of the finest art museums in the country.

The same year saw the first production at the Cleveland Play House, which has become the longest-running professional theater in the United States and the only institution of its kind that has been in continual operation since its establishment more than one hundred years ago. The Cleveland Playhouse was founded in 1915 by the Brooks and Drury families. The theater's first productions were staged in a vacant house that was owned by the Drurys and then moved to its first permanent home, a church on Cedar Avenue. In just four years, annual attendance at Playhouse productions grew from four thousand to forty thousand, and the theater company has been a success since then.

Culture in Cleveland took another leap in 1917 with the establishment of the Cleveland Metroparks System, a chain of parklands in Cuyahoga and Medina Counties that enabled Clevelanders the opportunity to reconnect with the land and escape the crowding of urban neighborhoods. The system's linked network of twelve park reservations surrounds the city. Cleveland's park district was conceived by William Stinchcomb, who was appointed to be its first director in 1921. Today, the park district includes nearly twenty thousand acres of parklands as well as the Cleveland Zoological Park and Aquarium.

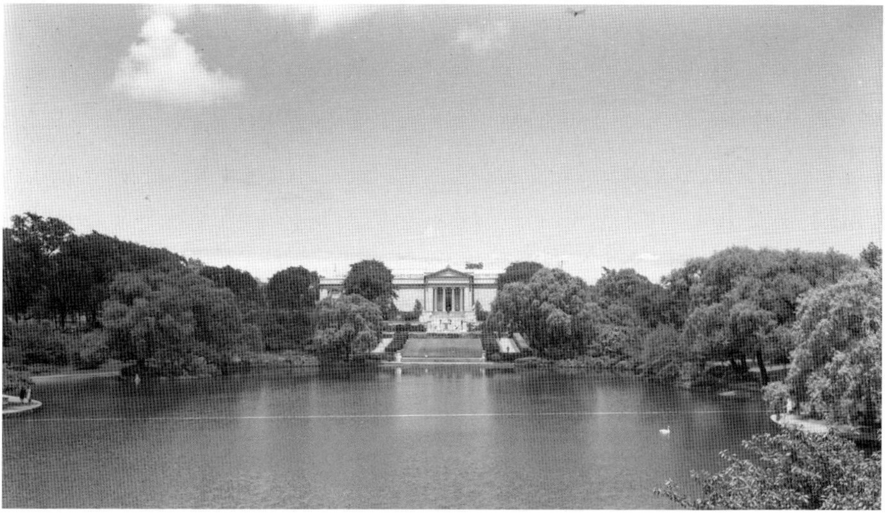

Exterior view of the Cleveland Museum of Art looking across the Wade Lagoon from the Fine Arts Garden at the northern end of Wade Park in Cleveland's University Circle area. *Schwartz.*

One year later, in 1918, the Cleveland Orchestra, now uniformly recognized as one of the world's finest, presented its first concert in Gray's Armory in the Cleveland suburb of Cleveland Heights. Over the next fifteen years, the orchestra presented its concerts at a succession of locations until 1931, when a gift from Mr. and Mrs. Jon L. Severence allowed the orchestra's Musical Arts Association to construct Severence Hall in the University Circle. In addition to the orchestra, the association supports the Cleveland Orchestra Chorus.

In 1920, the Cleveland Museum of Natural History was initiated by a group of civic leaders led by Harold Clark. Its first museum space was in the former Leonard Hanna mansion on Euclid Avenue. In the late 1950s, the museum moved to its present University Circle location on the Wade Park Oval. The museum is focused on providing educational programs on the natural world. To support its programs, the museum maintains a collection of more than 1 million specimens, including "Lucy," the earliest known hominid at the time of her discovery, as well as a collection of dinosaur skeletons and other natural specimens.

Progress in the sciences continued a year later, when the Cleveland Clinic was established. The Cleveland Clinic medical center was founded by a group of local physicians who had served together during World War I. The clinic suffered an early setback in 1929, when a fire in an area that housed nitrate-based X-ray films released poisonous fumes in the hospital and killed 123 people. This disaster and the stock market crash that occurred in the same year threatened to end the clinic's short history, but a group of prominent Clevelanders financially supported the clinic, leading to its survival and expansion after World War II. Through the years, doctors at the Cleveland Clinic have made important medical advancements in treating kidney disease and exploring the use of artificial organs, including the artificial kidney and the first successful larynx transplant.

Additional important work at the Cleveland Clinic included making advancements in cardiac care, including radical heart surgery and heart transplant. In addition to its direct medical care facilities, the clinic operates the largest postgraduate medical education program and was an early advocate of continuing medical education for practicing physicians. Today, the Cleveland Clinic covers a 140-square-block area that stretches from East 88th to the west to East 105th Street and University Circle to the east. The clinic is also famous for being the hospital of choice for many of the world's foreign heads of state, government officials, sports figures and celebrities. The Cleveland Clinic System also supports the community and the state by being Cleveland's largest and the state's third-largest employer.

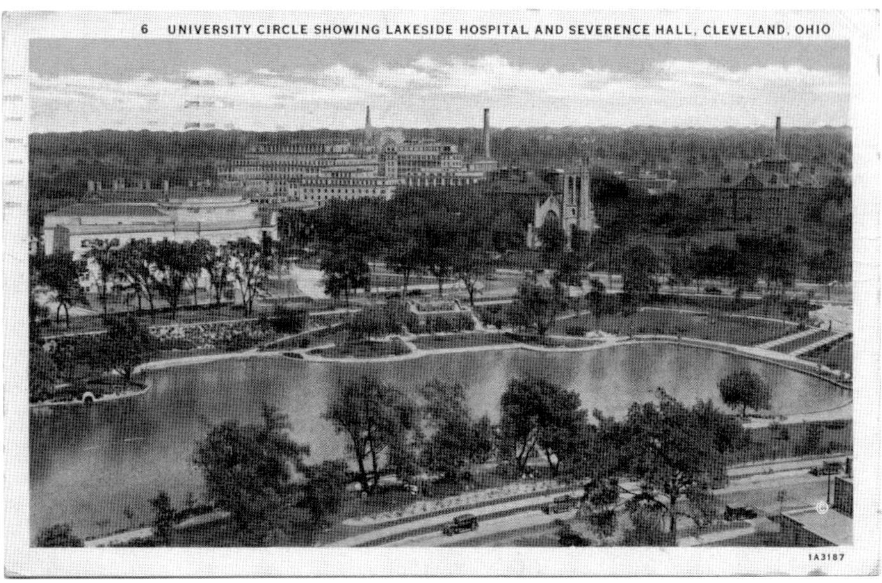

Aerial view of Wade Park in Cleveland, Ohio, looking southeast across Cleveland's University Circle area, showing Severance Hall and Lakeside Hospital buildings. *Cleveland Memory Project.*

In 1922, the age of radio came to Cleveland when station WHK became one of the nation's first six radio broadcasting stations. The station was started and owned by Warren R. Cox, and he operated it from his home as a hobby station for members of the Cleveland Radio Association. In 1922, the U.S. Department of Commerce made it unlawful to broadcast information to the public from an amateur radio station without a commercial license. Cox responded to this order by applying for a broadcaster's license and established the WHK station at the frequency of 1,420 kilocycles on the radio dial. Cox sold the station to the Radio Air Service Corporation in 1925, and it increased the station's power to five thousand watts for both day and night operations. In 1930, the WHK station joined the family of CBS stations, which aired recorded music, public speeches, sermons, news, concerts, interviews and weather reports. Also in 1922, one of the key Group Plan buildings, Cleveland's Public Auditorium, was dedicated as the largest convention hall in the nation. The Republican Party held its National Conventions at the Cleveland location in 1924 and 1936.

The size of the auditorium's convention hall led to Cleveland becoming one of the nation's leading convention centers. The building was planned before World War I, but like many other Group Plan elements, construction wasn't begun until 1920. The building's façade was designed in a classic Renaissance style by architect J.H. MacDowell with the assistance of architect Frank R. Walker. The hall's seating capacity was 11,500, and the basement exhibition hall provided more than 28,500 square feet of display space. The hall included a stage at one end, with a stage front that was seventy-two feet wide and forty-two feet high. The stage also included one of the world's largest pipe organs. In 1929, a music hall was added to the south end of the building. The back-to-back stages of the hall and the auditorium provided a unique location when the two halls were united into a single venue by raising a stage wall. An underground exhibition hall was constructed beneath the north end of the Mall and connected to the auditorium in 1932.

Cleveland's cultural footprint became larger in the same year when Cleveland's Palace Theater was opened. The theater, located on Cleveland's main street, Euclid Avenue, became the key location in Cleveland's Playhouse Square. The $3.5 million theater was designed by the Chicago architectural firm Rapp & Rapp as a vaudeville theater. The theater was a true palace, with white Carrera marble and more than thirty original paintings in its "Great Hall" lobby. The auditorium seated 3,100 patrons, and its stage was fifty-nine feet wide and ninety feet deep. Its backstage area housed elegant main dressing rooms, a billiard room, a barbershop, a nursery and a putting green. Shortly after it opened, the vaudeville era came to a close with the advent of motion pictures. In 1926, its vaudeville productions were dropped to accommodate the showing of motion pictures, with live entertainment interspersed between them, including performances by Bob Hope, and the marriage of George Burns and Gracie Allen.

In 1925, Cleveland's Main Public Library building, another Group Plan element, opened, partially enclosing the southern end of the Mall. The Main Library building, an adjoining building and its Eastman Reading Garden occupy an entire city block on Superior Avenue. The Cleveland Public Library dates back to 1869, when it opened as a public school library for the Cleveland Board of Education. It was the nation's first large public library that allowed patrons to select books directly from bookshelves. The library was in a succession of temporary rented spaces until the main library building was opened in 1925. By the early 1930s, more than twelve thousand people used the main library building every day. Also in 1925, the Cleveland Municipal Airport, now known as Cleveland Hopkins International Airport, opened eight miles south of the city. The idea of establishing an airport in Cleveland was originally conceived shortly after World War I, but it didn't become a reality until the federal government determined that the city would be able to provide adequate infrastructure for U.S. Air Mail planes on their coast-to-coast flights. In 1925, City Manager William Hopkins obtained the Cleveland City Council's permission to issue bonds to build the airport on 1,040 acres of land. The airport's first terminal building featured the world's first airport control tower. Cleveland's airport became famous for hosting the National Air Races, starting in 1929.

Cleveland in the Great Depression

The postwar 1920s were prosperous times in the nation's large cities. A lot of construction was being done in and around cities, and the population in cities was expanding. While industrial production was thriving and wages were increasing, the cost of living was rising faster that wages. Only 2 percent of Americans owned stock, but those who owned the stocks were those who were in control of the county's finances.

While Cleveland's extended period of advancements kept pushing on, there were signs, starting in 1927, that all was not well for an increasingly larger portion of the city's population. A groundswell of discontent among the less fortunate was matched by trouble at the top when the bills came due. Much of the nation's industrial and civic development had been leveraged against stock holdings, which grew rapidly until a series of checks to stock overvaluation occurred in 1929. Projects such as the Terminal Tower development had been financed with millions of dollars of loans against stock holdings, and when the stock market crashed, projects that had been based on artificially high stock valuations crashed along with them.

By 1931, two years after the Great Depression officially began, half of Cleveland's workers were unemployed. City aid workers hoped that this was going to be the peak of the downturn, but unfortunately that wasn't to be. Many of the unemployed who were unable to pay their rent or their taxes were evicted from their homes or faced foreclosures on their home loans. Unemployment continued to grow, and more men joined those who were already living in open areas on Cleveland's Whiskey Island and in Cleveland's lakefront city dump—areas that would become known as "Hoovervilles." The Associated Charities, a forerunner of the United Way group that was organized to assist Cleveland families during World War I,

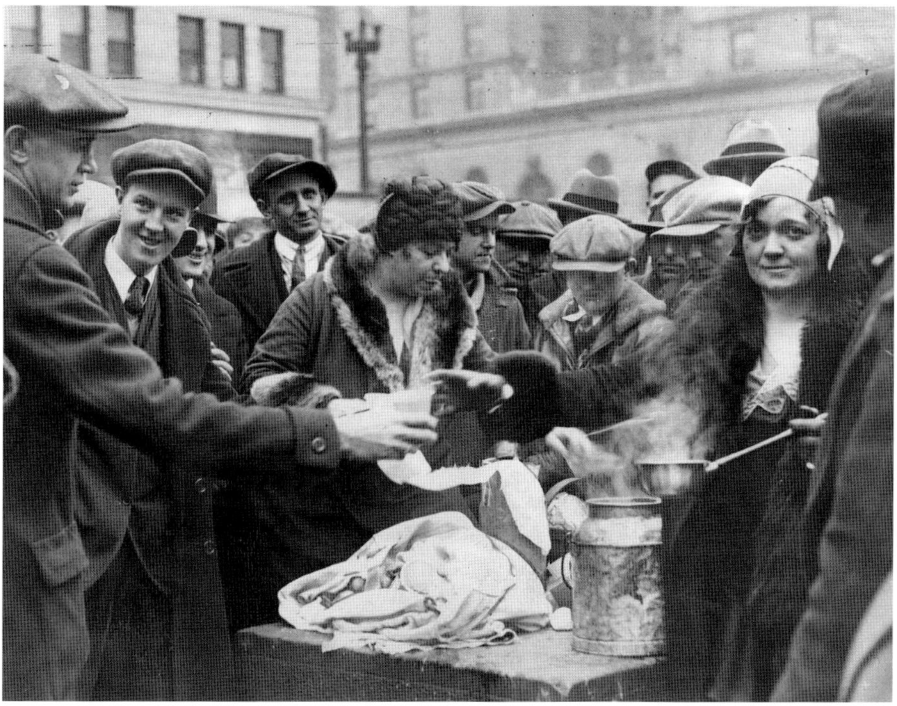

Cleveland's unemployed gather in Public Square to receive hot coffee and rolls as part of an aid effort by Cleveland restaurants. *Cleveland Memory Project.*

had organized a city works program that was paying men sixty cents per hour to work on building roads and sanitation projects, but it was quickly running out of money. Relief payments also overwhelmed the federal Works Project Administration, which was employing workers to build roads, schools, bridges and parks. By 1933, a total of nearly 220,000 of the nation's workers were unemployed, 77,000 families were receiving government assistance and a run on the banks threatened to severely and possible irreversibly damage the country's financial system.

By 1934, wages and working condition strikes were almost constant, including workers' strikes against Cleveland's steel mills and automobile manufacturers. Civil unrest, political corruption, communist and socialist leanings and riots continued to make the situation worse in Cleveland and in other cities, and in 1934, the National Communist Convention was held in Cleveland. The Van Sweringen brothers, creators of Cleveland's Union Terminal Tower complex, were also victims of the economic downturn. Their Shaker Heights had been an instant success. From 1919 to 1929, Shaker's population had grown tenfold, but several of the nine railroads that the brothers had acquired had gone bankrupt and both brothers died shortly after.

THE GREAT LAKES EXPOSITION

The Great Lakes Exposition was held in Cleveland, Ohio, during the Great Depression summers of 1936 and 1937. The purpose of the exposition was to commemorate the centennial of Cleveland's incorporation as a city in 1836 and celebrate the industrial riches of the Great Lakes states. The exposition was organized by a small group of Cleveland business leaders who in just four months raised $1.1 million in loaned investments to develop the exposition grounds. There was little time to pull the exposition together, and in just eighty days, thousands of Cleveland's building trade workers and additional hundreds of men who were employed through the federal government's Works Progress Administration completed the work of installing utilities, paving roads and plazas and constructing the exposition's more than 150 buildings and features. During its first summer, the exposition drew just under 4 million visitors; in its second summer, it drew another 3.5 million. The 1930s was the age of expositions. Chicago staged the Century of Progress International Exposition from 1933 to 1934, San Diego had its California Pacific International Exposition from 1935 to 1936, Dallas hosted the Texas Centennial Exposition in 1936, San Francisco staged the Golden Gate International Exposition from 1939 to 1940 and New York hosted the New York World's Fair from 1939 to 1940.

June 1936 proved to be a busy month in Cleveland. Long before the expo's organizers conceived their plan to open their grand show on June 27, the city had committed to hosting the 1936 Republican National Convention June 9–12. A few weeks before the exposition opened, Cleveland hosted the convention that nominated Alfred Landon and Frank Knox to be the Republican presidential and vice-presidential candidates.

The Great Lakes Exposition occupied a 135-acre site that included much of the area in the city's downtown core and along its lakefront that had been committed to the development of the Group Plan. In the mid-1930s, the land that was intended to house Burnham's Great Mall was vacant and strewn with rubble from buildings that had been demolished in preparation for its construction. Additional land for the exposition grounds was assembled from derelict parcels along Cleveland's Lake Erie shoreline that were home to a desperate army of Depression-era homeless men. In addition to these downtown and lakeshore properties, the exposition was granted the use of $40 million worth of Cleveland's existing building and land assets, including the Public Auditorium on the eastern edge of the Mall area and Cleveland's Municipal Stadium along Cleveland's lakefront.

A historical plus for the city was that for the duration of the exposition—and for the first time in its history—Cleveland's downtown and its lakefront were linked by a wooden causeway built over the lakeshore railroad frontage that had separated since the rail lines were laid down fifty years earlier. Only a few of the more than 150 buildings constructed for the exposition were meant to be permanent, and eighty years after the expo's two-year run, nothing of the exposition remains. Cleveland's Great Lakes Science Center, the Rock and Roll Hall of Fame and Museum, the Cleveland Browns' First Energy Field and Burke Lakefront Airport now occupy the land where the exposition stood during the summers of 1936 and 1937.

Visitors to the expo entered the grounds by passing under seventy-seven-foot-tall pylons that would become the expo's iconic image. Visitors then moved through the Sherwin-Williams Plaza and the Court of the Great Lakes. The Sherwin-Williams Plaza housed the Sherwin-Williams Bandshell, where the nation's top big bands performed daily, and the Court of the Great Lakes housed a variety of displays that highlighted the history and future of the Great Lakes states. Cleveland's Public Hall, where the

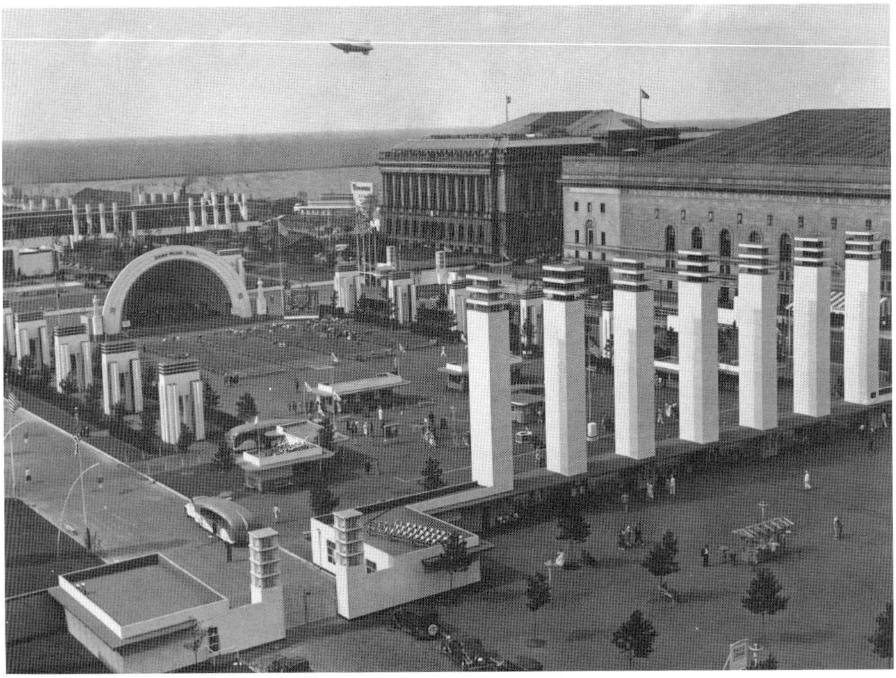

Visitors to the Great Lakes Exposition entered the grounds through the main entrance on St. Clair Avenue. The entrance's seven towers became one of the expo's iconic images. *Cleveland Memory Project.*

Republican National Convention was held, was adjacent to the plaza, and during the expo, it was home to the world's largest radio broadcasting studio and other displays that demonstrated the leading innovations of the day. From an overlook at the north end of the court, exposition visitors got their first view of the lower portions of the grounds. The Court of the Presidents, which occupied the wooden causeway that was built for the exposition to span Cleveland's lakeshore railway system, was bordered by sixteen sixteen-foot-high pillars that were topped by sixteen-foot-high gilded eagles. Each pillar had a plaque that honored a U.S. president who was either born in or was elected from a Great Lakes state. The court also housed one hundred booths on its east and west edges where visitors could buy food and souvenirs.

At the northern end of the causeway was the Standard Drug Building, where the Court of the Presidents transitioned to the Marine Plaza. The Marine Plaza had a broad grassy infield bordered by tall masts with illuminated "crow's nests" and lines of colorful flags. The plaza's attractions

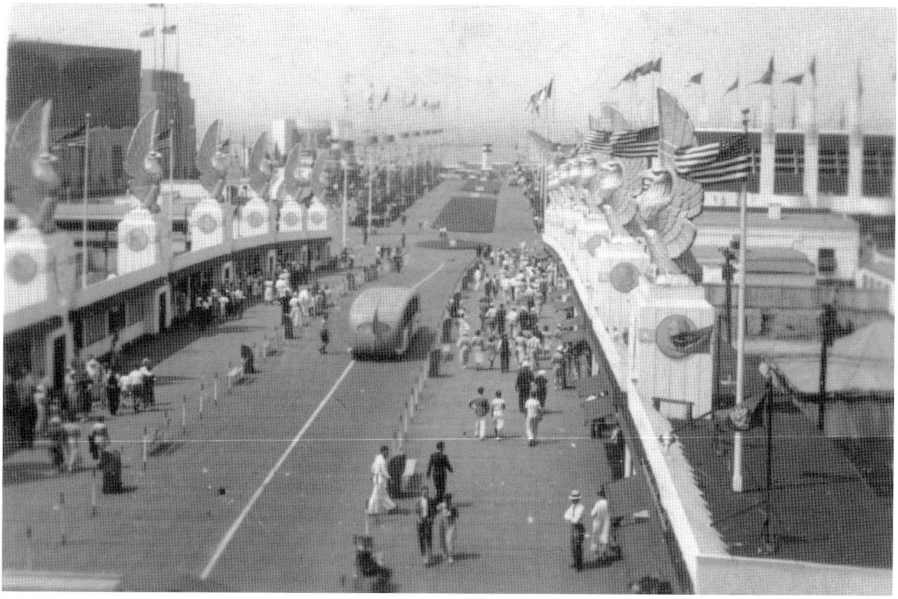

The exposition's Court of the Presidents spanned the city's lakeshore railway and provided, for the first time, a physical link between Cleveland's downtown and its Lake Erie shoreline. *Schwartz.*

included the Hall of Progress, where the epic production "Parade of the Years" was staged; the Automotive Building, in which the most impressive automotive industry advancements were displayed; the Hall of Progress, where exhibits of public service and other industries were presented; the Enamel Building, which housed displays of some of the most advanced technologies that existed at the time; and Cleveland's Municipal Stadium, where a stunning variety of professional and amateur athletic events was offered, including soccer, track and field meets, ski jumping, archery tournaments and many other sporting events. The Cleveland Indians moved from their home field at League Park on Cleveland's east side to Municipal Stadium and played games there for the first time during the exposition's two seasons.

To the west on the plaza, visitors could visit the only two of the expo's features meant to be permanent additions to Cleveland's lakefront: the nautical-themed Horticulture Building and the one-thousand-foot-long Horticultural Gardens. Also to the west were a floating New York–style nightclub on the converted steamship *Moses Cleaveland* and a large hillside floral depiction of the exposition's logo. To the east on the Marine Plaza were the ultramodern Art Deco–styled Transportation Building, the Firestone Building and the Singing Fountains.

Exposition visitors then continued to the east, where they encountered the expo's Amusement and Midway sections. These sections included attractions that reflected both the good and bad aspects of the culture of 1930s America. In the Amusement section, visitors could have their photograph taken (still a rare event for most people in the 1930s), see a circus, watch a Shakespearean play in a full-size reproduction of the Globe Theater or tour Admiral Richard E. Byrd's polar expedition ship, the *City of New York*. They could also descend into a World War I submarine, catch a fish dinner in an elevated pond, dance, go for a motorboat ride on the lake, ride over the expo grounds and downtown Cleveland in one of four Goodyear blimps or watch a fireworks display.

At the east end of the Midway, visitors encountered the castle-like entrance to the expo's Streets of the World (SOTW) section. This section celebrated the cultures, crafts, music, dance and food of nearly forty countries. In addition to these tamer features, the Streets of the World section also offered entertainment that would be socially inappropriate in today's world—in a nod to the success of similar attractions at the nation's previous expositions, many of the SOTW section's attractions featured female nudity.

Because the exposition did not meet its financial goals during the first summer, the decision was made to reopen it the following summer. When the expo reopened at the end of May 1937, its monumental main entrance on St. Clair Avenue had been replaced by a smaller entrance on Lakeside Avenue, and some of its financially less successful and less socially appropriate attractions were replaced by larger, more phenomenal and more appropriate features. One of the 1937 additions was a huge floating stage and a lake-water pool that featured Billy Rose's Aquacade—a music, dance and swimming show that starred Johnny Weissmuller of Tarzan fame and Olympic gold medalist Eleanor Holm. Although it was forbidden by exposition organizers during the second year, a few of the expo's 1937 attractions tried off and on to draw people in by offering female nudity, but their efforts were quickly checked.

Some of the more than 180 photographs that the author's father produced when he was working for the White Motors Corporation in the summer 1936 highlight the exposition's architecture and grandeur, but a number of his images show the grittiness and desperation of the Great Depression as well.

Attending the exposition required a financial commitment, especially for economically challenged Depression-era Americans. As seen in period

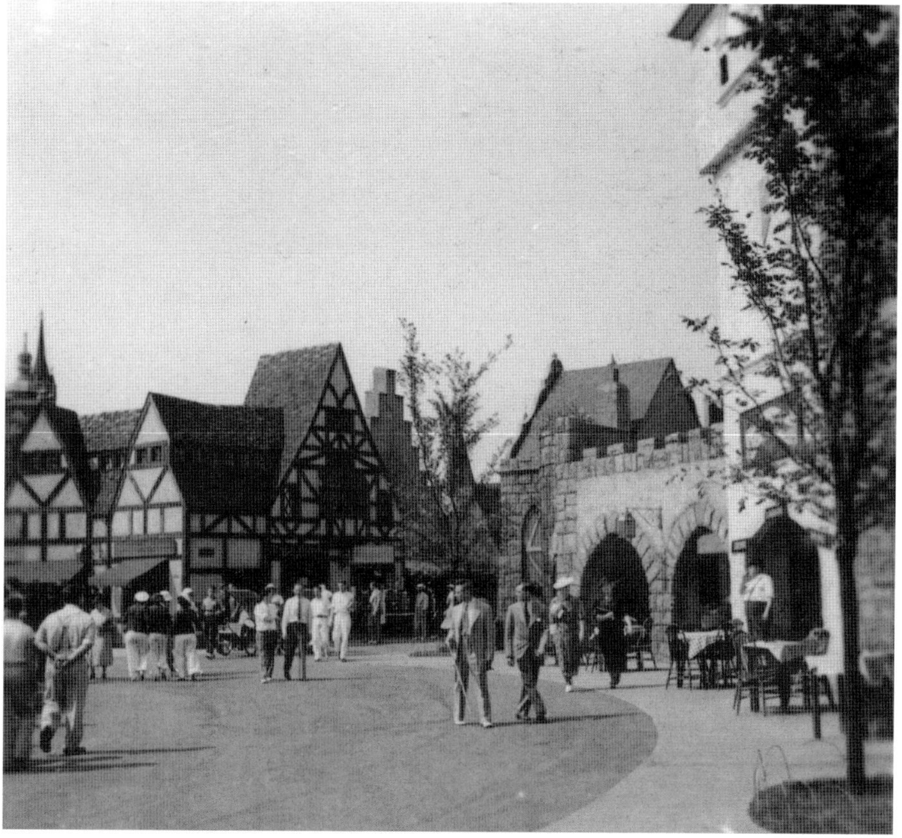

Well-dressed visitors to the Great Lakes Exposition stroll through the expo's Streets of the World section, which was designed by Cleveland-based theater designer Richard Rychtarik. *Schwartz.*

photographs, nearly all of the exposition's attendees were well-dressed and well-off Caucasians. Partly because it was the 1930s and partly because the exposition was an "event," the adopted dress code for the expo included summer dresses and heels for women and jackets and ties for men. There were very few children in attendance, especially during its first year, when nudity and questionable entertainment abounded. Nearly all of the expo's attractions required a separate entrance fee of between \$0.15 to see the Monkey Circus on the Midway to \$3 to ride in a Goodyear blimp. Depending on how much one chose to do and eat, and how many souvenirs purchased, the cost for one day at the expo could range from \$6 to \$15, equal to \$100 to \$250 in today's dollars—about the cost of a one-day ticket at Walt Disney World.

While Cleveland's Great Lakes Exposition was not a financial success, the expo drew positive national attention to an industrial city that had been ravaged by the disinvestment and crime that accompanied the Great Depression, and Cleveland showed that it could rise and meet its challenges. The legacy of the Great Lakes Exposition and the site on which it was held is a mixed one. The summer of 1936 was abnormally hot, the abundance of nudity at many of the attractions and the price of admission kept families and the less wealthy away and the expo did not draw many repeat visitors—all factors that negatively affected revenues. Even after an additional year of operation, investors received back only half of their loaned investments.

THE WORLD IN THE 1930S

As for the world in the mid-1930s, change was everywhere and political tensions were high. The winter and summer Olympics were both held in Germany, the Hoover Dam was completed, Nazi Germany violated international treaties and reoccupied the Rhineland, Richard Hauptman was executed after being convicted of the Lindbergh kidnapping in 1932, Italian military forces occupied Ethiopia, a major heat wave brought widespread death to North America and reduced exposition attendance, *Gone with the Wind* was published (and adapted as a film), the first fully controllable helicopter made its maiden voyage, the Spanish Civil War commenced, the British Broadcasting Corporation launched the world's first viable television broadcasts, Franklin Roosevelt was reelected to a second term as president of the United States, the first edition of *LIFE* magazine was published, Edward VIII abdicated the English throne and—a few years after the exposition closed its gates—the world was again at war.

Also in 1936, fluorescent lighting was introduced at Cleveland's NELA (an acronym for the National Electric Lamp Association) Park. NELA Park was one of the nation's earliest, and possibly the first, industrial research parks. The park was conceived by officers of the National Electric Lamp Company, which soon became the lamp division of the General Electric Company. In a nod to the past, the research facility featured English and colonial architecture, and the construction techniques that were used at NELA Park became standards for industrial construction. The facility also featured sophisticated mechanical systems and underground utility tunnels. NELA Park's campus has been described as being "a perfect representation

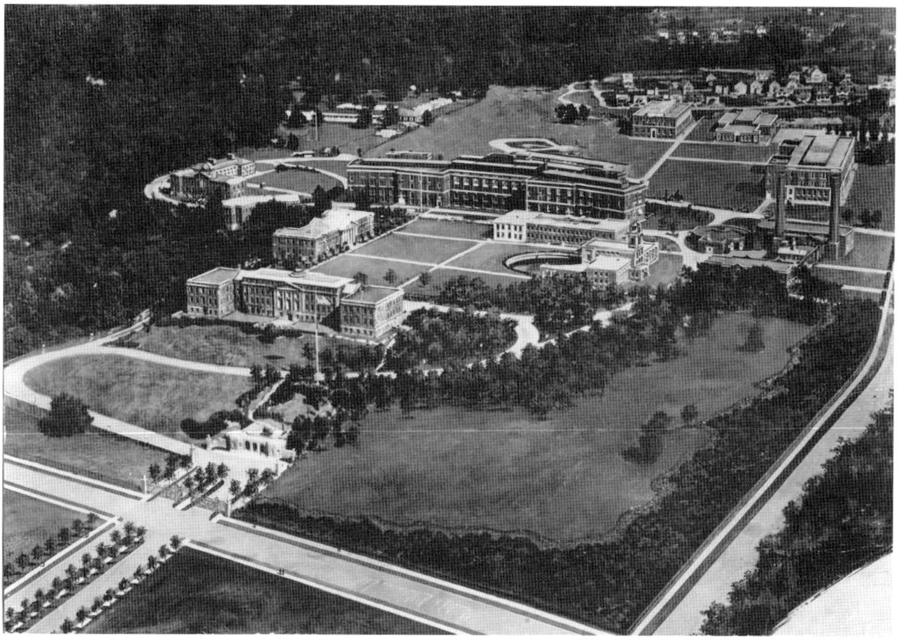

Aerial view of buildings and park areas in Cleveland's NELA Park industrial development. NELA Park's campus adopted a City Beautiful–inspired design ethic. *Case Western Reserve University.*

of the early 20th-century academic ideal." Art and sculpture are also represented on the NELA Park campus, including a seventy-two-foot-tall bell tower and a bronze statuary group symbolizing the triumph of light over darkness. In many ways, the NELA Park embodied many City Beautiful design ideals.

Post-Depression Cleveland

Millions of U.S. workers lost their jobs during the Depression, and by 1932, nearly one-fourth of America's families had meager means of income. As a state that was heavily industrialized, Ohio was hit very hard by the Great Depression. By 1933, more than 40 percent of Ohio's factory workers and 67 percent of its construction workers were unemployed. Employment conditions were even worse in Cleveland, with 50 percent of its industrial workers and more than 35 percent of its total worker population being unemployed. Many workers who were still employed were working fewer hours per week for a lower wage, which made it harder to support their families. President Roosevelt's New Deal programs and federal banking controls were created to respond to these conditions. By the end of the 1930s, because of these programs and industrial production that began in response to another looming world war, Cleveland and the rest of the country had begun to recover, and by the early 1940s, the Great Depression had come to an end. Like the 1920s, the 1940s were again prosperous times in America's cities, but problems that were fostered before and during the Depression persisted, including increasing racial tensions and the flight of Caucasians to the suburbs. Cleveland's prosperity in the 1940s brought even more people to the city, and by 1950, Cleveland's population had risen to an all-time high of 915,000.

The postwar 1920s were a prosperous and vibrant time for industrial cities. Rapid industrial and manufacturing growth brought more people to Cleveland from southern states and from eastern Europe. This influx of people fueled additional growth and additional challenges. The city did its best to respond to the needs of its citizens and created infrastructure, parks and welfare and benevolent institutions to respond to their needs. Housing was developed at a record pace, and Cleveland was immersed in the Jazz Age. In 1920, the Cleveland Indians defeated the Brooklyn Robins in the World Series, and the city was looking forward to an uninterrupted period of development and advancement.

It Could Have Been Different

The City Beautiful movement's ideals were focused on making small portions of cities' central cores look better by applying a design ethic that looked back to Neoclassical styles. The movement's proponents thought that positive change could be brought about by changing a city's physical face but gave no thought to addressing social issues that were directly affecting the quality of life of a city's inhabitants. It is impossible to know if the problems that negatively affected America's economy in the late 1920s could have been altered if more of the people who could have made a difference had recognized that bad times were ahead and had taken measures that would have made a difference before the Great Depression broke out.

Upton Sinclair and social scientists raised red flags twenty years before the economy started to bottom out in the late 1920s, but they had no sway over those who had the means to make the kind of economic changes that needed to be made early in the century to avert what happened. It might have been impossible for the country and the world to have taken a step back and have the foresight to stand in the way of what they saw as progress and put effort into bringing about progress in making lasting social change alongside short-term economic progress. Yet real change in America's cities might have been possible if social scientists had been included in the City Beautiful movement's design teams. Maybe then the result could have been beautiful cities where people could live in a place that had great "curb appeal" and that allowed them to feel secure in their homes.

A Vision Interrupted

It does not do to leave a dragon out of your calculations, if you live near him.
—J.R.R. Tolkien, The Hobbit

The first decades of a new century always bring significant change. The years from 1890 to 1930 were as dramatic as any other time. Formal Edwardian ideals ran headlong into new progressive thinking born out of an unprecedented technological revolution and a newly empowered feminist movement. It was during this time that powers in Cleveland decided to clean house and create a downtown worthy of the city's new status in the world. Creating a great downtown is not easy. Creating a downtown that is meant to impress visitors and change the attitudes and lives of the citizens living there is a monumental task.

At the beginning of the twentieth century, the Cleveland city fathers hired a team of planners to create a vision for downtown Cleveland. In 1903, the plan was presented by architects Arnold W. Brunner, John M. Carrére and Daniel Burnham. The concept was elegant and simple in its layout. The clean European lines and majestic Mall envisioned by these men were well received by the city's fathers. Unfortunately, the execution of the plan would be fraught with complications of unpredictable scope and origins over the coming years. These Tolkien-like dragons all had the common effect of upending and delaying the civic and commercial plans for creating a grand, orderly and European-inspired downtown environment in Cleveland. While the concepts of the City Beautiful movement were noble in intent, the reality of trying to execute such a large scope of work (as in the Group Plan) proved problematic. The concept of the Group Plan would be implemented in fits and starts that would stretch over almost a century.

The original six buildings of the Group Plan that remain today took twenty-seven years to be built from the 1903 starting date. The original plan, despite being organized with a holistic approach, was burdened with turn-of-the-century tastes and concepts at its core. The European monumental wide-open public mall embodied in the Group Plan had its critics. Many prominent architects felt that a more American approach was needed for the major cities. The critical years surrounding and including the decade of the 1920s presented unprecedented hurtles and obstacles to the world and, thus, to the City of Cleveland's Group Plan.

All the associated downtown improvements and developments would evolve more naturally as tastes and technology changed over time. The great cities such as Paris and London were built over centuries. They accumulated their magnificent parks and buildings through many leaders and architects on step at a time. Cleveland was attempting a sort of wholesale change, wiping the table clean and starting from scratch in what would normally be a blink of an eye in the life of a great city.

Despite the Great War, the Great Depression, the Dust Bowl and Prohibition, industrial boom and bust experienced in the 1910s through 1930s, downtown Cleveland pushed through and out came a great downtown from the other side. Downtown has its public mall and monumental buildings, but even better, it has its own distinct flavor and personality that is undeniably Cleveland.

SOCIETY AND POLITICS CHANGE THE FACE OF CLEVELAND

The ways of the Victorian era and, even more prominently, the Edwardian era crashed directly into the burgeoning progressive modern industrial age the United States was experiencing in the early decades of the twentieth century. Downtown Cleveland was heavily populated with hundreds of creaky, dusty, dated Victorian buildings built in the mid- to late 1800s during a surge in downtown Cleveland. Internal plumbing, furnaces, electricity and telephones were generally not conceived at the time of their construction. The buildings with mansard roofs and ornate gables built in the late 1800s did not sit well with monumental Beaux-Arts–style structures being constructed in downtown Cleveland. Even the grand homes on Euclid Avenue that comprised "Millionaires' Row" started to decline in about 1910. Many of the older structures that lined West Third Street and Lakeside Avenue appeared to be merely large houses or mansions and were by then being used as hotels, boardinghouses and speakeasies. Decrepit old two- and three-story commercial buildings were standing next to monumental new government buildings, creating a symbol of old and new that would not last very long. The timeworn, sometimes leaning wooden structures would fall to the wrecking ball by the hundreds in the coming years.

The list of forces molding Cleveland's streets, businesses and culture was staggering. Staid Edwardian society and ideals were challenged after World War I by America's youth, who wanted a more progressive and exciting era. Rural America started a great movement into the cities to find jobs. Women achieved a foothold in the workplace during World War I and never let go. The birth of consumerism can be found in the 1920s. The economy was booming, and Cleveland was growing at a remarkable rate. The modes of transportation changed from the horse and buggy to the various forms of electric, gas and steam automobile, and mass transportation grew in the form of interurban streetcars. The flow of residents away from downtown

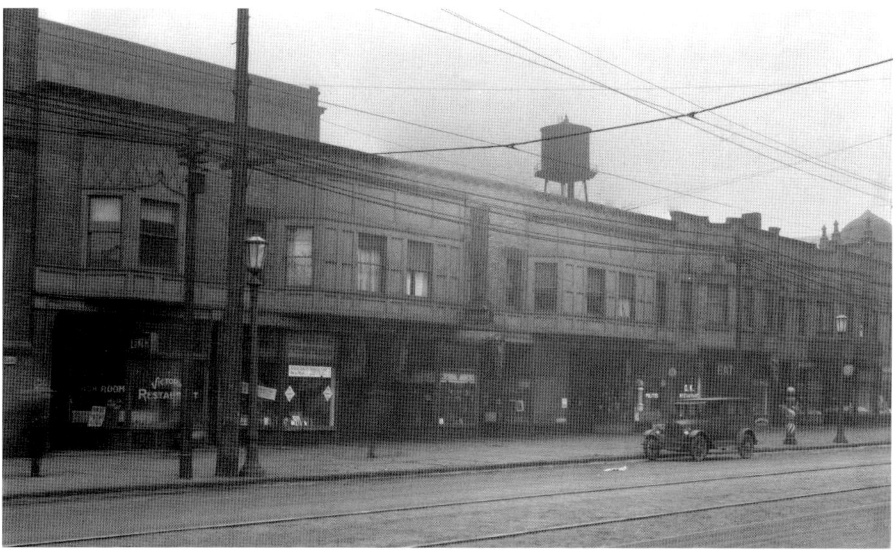

Situated on Ninth Street between St. Clair Avenue and Oregon Avenue, Tidd the tailor, the Victory Restaurant and Polito's Barbershop competed with the glitzy Euclid Avenue stores for customers. *Schwartz*.

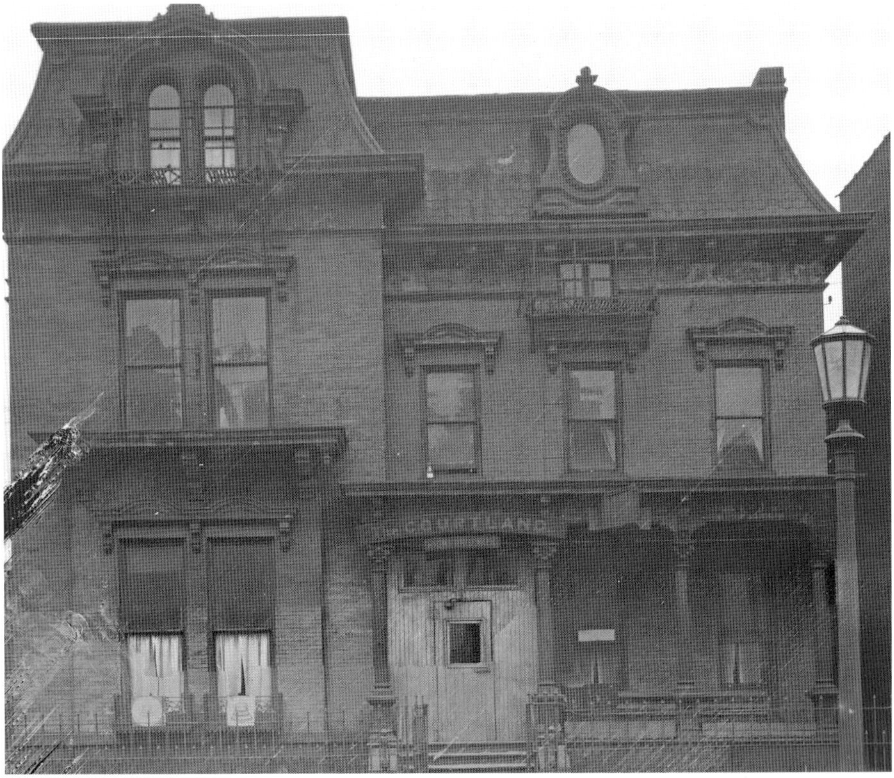

The Courtland Hotel circa 1925 on the corner of Ontario Street and Lakeside Avenue. *Schwartz.*

would slowly increase in the late 1920s and 1930s, from near downtown to the suburbs or the "Heights" on the east side.

The concept originating in the mid-1800s of living near or in the downtown area was abandoned after the turn of the century. The automobile and trolley allowed people to commute from the outskirts of town and get away from the dirt and grittiness of living next to small industry and the horse stalls of teamsters. By the early 1930s, even the opulent Victorian mansions on nearby Euclid Avenue were being used for commercial purposes such as car lots and small apartments. Many multipurpose buildings were erected to house stores on the ground floor and apartments above. The flow eastward of the middle class stemmed the tide of multi-unit residences in downtown Cleveland and ushered in the wrecking ball for most of them by 1930. With the decay of the older structures downtown, people began to move outward from the city center. Large modern apartment buildings were built on the edges of the downtown, further pulling residents outward. Suburban life took hold and did not let go until the gentrification of downtown almost one hundred years later.

In 1920, Cleveland was the fifth-largest city in the country, with a population of 796,841. That is an increase of 263,208 people (or 42 percent) from 560,633 in a mere ten years. Cleveland was feeling its oats and wanted to prove its status in the hierarchy of American cities. Cleveland flexed its urban muscles, powered by the heavy industry that filled the southern side of the city. The run-down or obsolete buildings were quickly marked for demolition and then torn down. There was a short time during the mid-1920s when lone structures would stand next to monumental newer buildings, further illustrating the inevitability of the time left for the pitiful few.

The Great War

The Great War, World War I, concluded in Europe in 1918 with the help of American troops. The war proved to be a catalyst of change on the coming decade of the 1920s. Wars always advance technological change much quicker than during peacetime. Soldiers, after traveling across the world and seeing strange and exotic sights, were not content to stay at home and work on the farm or in small towns. These changes in attitudes along with more cosmopolitan ideas transferred back to the States and to Cleveland.

Cleveland flexed its industrial muscles, and its output grew from sixth to fifth in the nation during the war. Cleveland's White Motor Corporation produced eighteen thousand trucks and ambulances for the war effort. The famous Thompson submachine gun was developed in Cleveland by Theodore Eickhoff for the Warner and Swasey Company. Cleveland also contributed the secretary of war, Newton D. Baker, a onetime mayor of the city. Advances in vehicles and transportation affected the downtown area by allowing for the concept of commuting to take hold. Interurban trains and trolleys proliferated. Cars evolved from just being toys for the rich to becoming affordable modes of transportation for the middle class.

During the war, there was a tremendous clash of nineteenth- and twentieth-century technologies—the horse versus the automobile, the telephone invading the confines of the home and plumbing moving indoors. Inventors were furiously turning out all kinds of creative gadgets and materials. Huge strides were made in radio communication, cars, planes, personal hygiene, medical techniques and, of course, lethal killing devices. All these developments had effects on the homefront. It was sometimes said that the world had gone as far as it could technologically.

Ohio experienced a drought of men as it sent 200,000 soldiers to the war in Europe. Cleveland provided 41,000 fighting men, with 1,023 making the ultimate sacrifice. Cleveland's Lakeside Hospital provided the first medical contingent with a staff of surgeons and nurses. Women were drawn into the workplace to fill jobs that would have been considered unconventional at the time. This helped to start to break down the societal barriers to women holding such jobs. Women still had a long way to go in job equality, but service jobs that were perceived as appropriate for women also boomed in the 1920s. Telephone operators, streetcar conductors, stenographers, receptionists and more were in great demand as the economy took off in the 1920s. The new woman was born. Most of these jobs were in the cities. The manpower shortage was also partially alleviated with the migration of African Americans from the South. The city's black population grew 300 percent in the years surrounding the war.

Cleveland at the time of the war had a large population of German and Hungarian immigrants. Many of the local Germans were sympathetic to the German side of the war. The Cleveland Public School system even went so far as to stop teaching the German language. This began the Americanization of immigrants, who did not want to be ostracized because of their country of origin.

Even with the return of soldiers, there was a labor shortage. The industrial might of America, and Cleveland in particular, was on a roll. Automobile factories were popping up in the heartland from Detroit to Pittsburgh. Cleveland was one of the first great auto manufacturing cities. By 1930, Cleveland had become home to more than thirty different automobile makers. The Great War created the final separation from old-world ideas and mores and set the stage in America for what would become the progressive Roaring Twenties.

INDUSTRIAL BOOM

In the early 1920s, the industrial boom gained steam in Cleveland. Workers were needed in the large factories in and around Cleveland. Steel and autos were the big players in heavy industry in Cleveland, which was in a battle with Detroit for car production. Cleveland had a head start, with many small car companies formed in the late 1800s and early 1900s. In 1909, automobile manufacturing ranked as the third-largest industry in the city, with thirty factories employing seven thousand people. The first car to be driven across the country was a Cleveland-built Winton in 1903. Cleveland car lovers also had the foresight to create the first auto club in 1900.

Despite the early efforts by Cleveland, Detroit exhibited an aggressive effort in building extremely large automobile factory complexes and would quickly win out over Cleveland. Detroit's success also hinged on specifically targeting middle-class lower-cost cars. Cleveland produced higher-end car models. Cleveland would be second in the United States only to Detroit in the number of automobiles and parts produced. Some of the bigger automakers unique to Cleveland included Chandler, Baker, Jordan, Cleveland, Winton, White and Peerless. Eighty different makes of automobiles were made in Cleveland up to 1931. This plethora of Cleveland automakers had many firsts. White Motors would move the handbrake inside the vehicle and innovate the transmission shifter. The horn button on the steering wheel, glass-sealed headlights, shock absorbers to smooth out the ride and probably many more inventions and ideas came from the many Cleveland automakers.

The industrial footprint helped shape the location of downtown. The factories of Cleveland would nestle right up to the downtown area to receive raw materials from the Cuyahoga River. Downtown Cleveland was ensconced between the industrial river and Lake Erie. The Cleveland city center would follow the path of least resistance and grow east and west using Euclid, Superior and Lakeside Avenues as conduits. There were also many small manufacturers that also needed labor. The printers, electroplaters, textile workers, hat makers and the service industry created a great demand on the workforce. These small factories were spread throughout the downtown streets. This contributed to the chaotic function of downtown as factories, garages, offices and residences all comingled in an unsupervised quilt of urban energy.

People moved from the nearby small towns and farms in droves to feed the industrial demand. Cleveland grew dramatically in the early twentieth century. The city absorbed these workers readily. To feed the hungry workers, small diners and kitchens appeared on just about every corner of downtown. The service industry boomed to include barbers, dentists and any other service people would need.

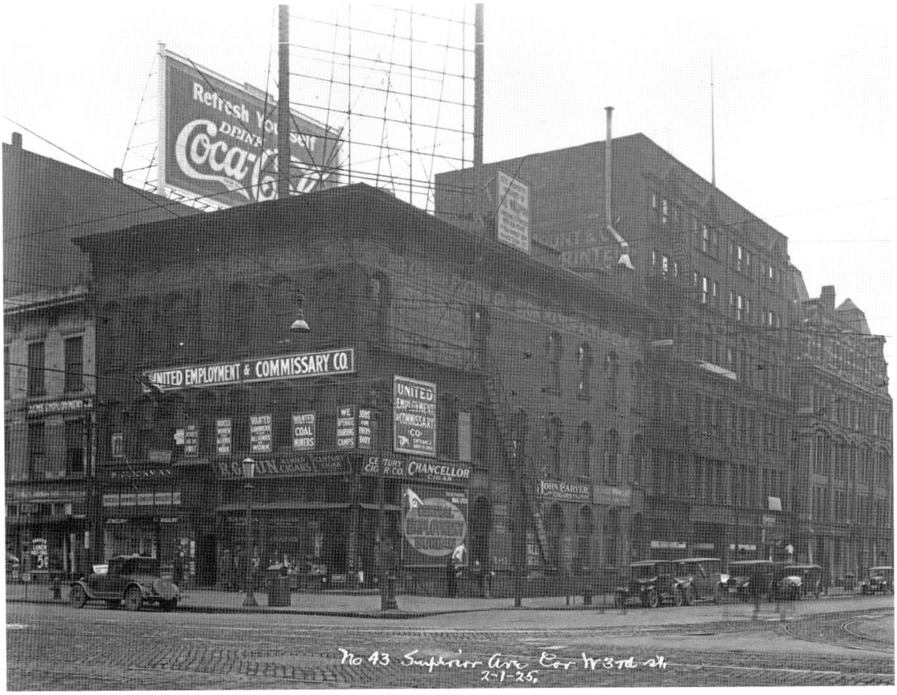

The corner of Superior Avenue and West Third Street, 1925. Employment agencies proliferated. *Schwartz.*

Similar to today, technology was moving so fast that it was hard for the factories to keep up. Gramophone makers quickly gave way to radio for entertainment. Soon, electric-powered radios and hand-crank record players were combined into what was called "orthophonic" sound machines, powered by electricity. Many of these new home entertainment combinations were placed in fine cabinetry and sold in furniture stores. The Jazz Age fueled the interest in these newfangled entertainment machines. Buggy whip manufacturers disappeared as auto mechanics and garages populated the streets. Gas pumps were planted right on the curbs in downtown. Traffic control was a problem. There were only mechanical stop-and-go signs operated by hand during peak traffic times. Pedestrians, horses and automobiles fought for supremacy on the downtown streets. This surge in innovation was unprecedented in history.

It is estimated that 500,000 African Americans migrated north from 1910 to 1930. The industrial jobs and a modicum of freedom created an irresistible pull on rural southern populations. This contributed to the changing face of Cleveland's many ethnic neighborhoods. In 1920, African Americans made up only 3 percent of Ohio's population; their numbers had increased dramatically to 5 percent of the population by 1930.

GARRETT MORGAN

Garrett Morgan (1877–1963) was a Cleveland inventor of necessity. When he saw firemen struggling to breathe when rescuing people in smoky environments, he created the first practical gas mask. When he observed a serious car accident in downtown Cleveland, he decided to create a mechanical traffic signal to alleviate the issue of horses, cars and people all trying to negotiate the busy streets of downtown. Morgan's traffic signal was one of the first to introduce a third signal that stopped all traffic all ways and then let one direction proceed. This helped make downtown Cleveland much safer for pedestrians and horses alike. Morgan was also

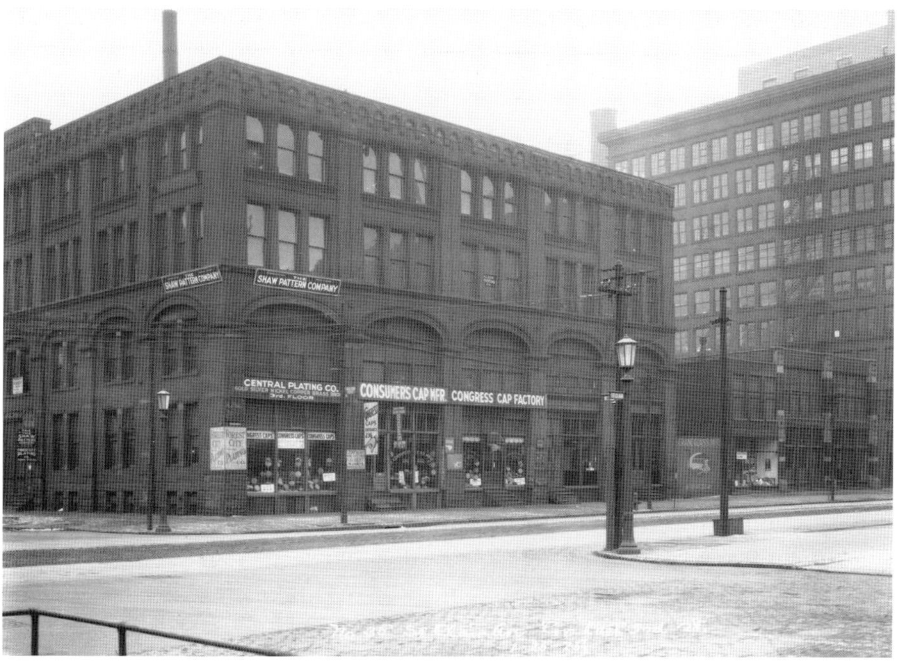

The Central Plating Company, Shaw Pattern Company, Consumers Cap, Forest City Plating, Congress Cap Factory, Watt Printing and Klein Printing resided at St. Clair Avenue and East Third Street in 1925. *Schwartz.*

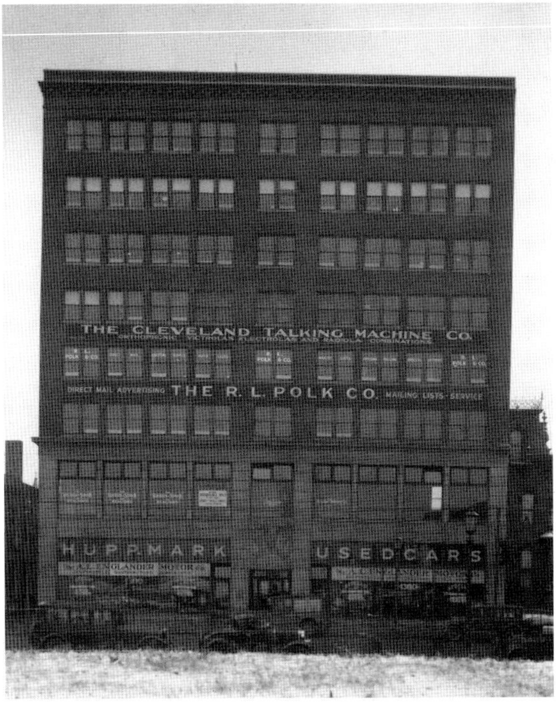

Left: The Cleveland Talking Machine Company building, at 4300 Euclid Avenue, was the primary distributer for the Victor Talking Machine Company in Cleveland.

Below: Kaffee Hag or decaf sign over the Colonial Restaurant, corner of East Sixth Street and St. Clair Avenue, circa 1925. *Schwartz*.

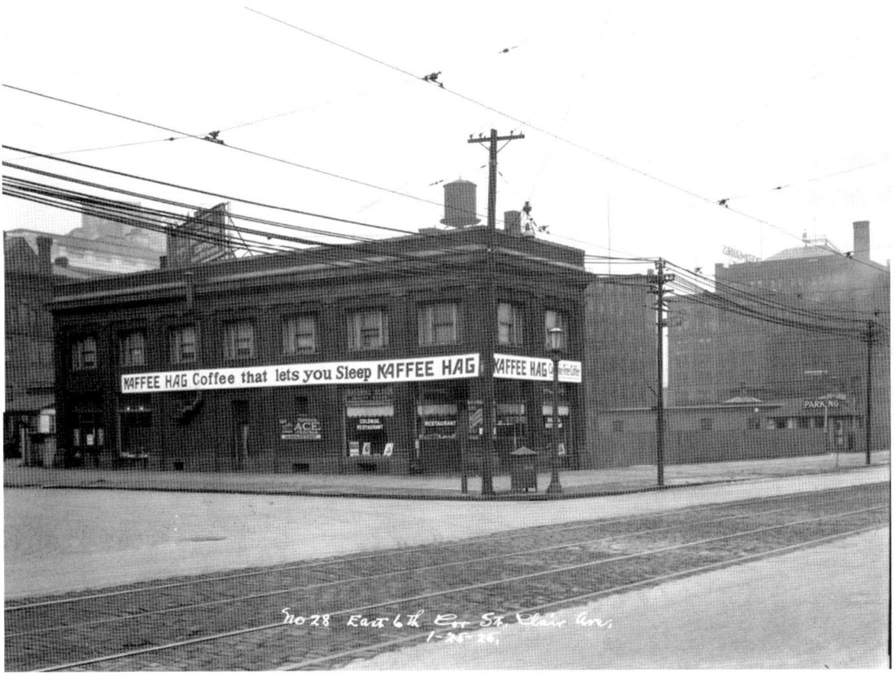

the first African American person to own a car in Cleveland. Being African American in the 1920s, his accomplishments tended to be overlooked. He did receive a gold medal award from the International Association of Fire Chiefs for his gas mask. Cleveland named the Garrett A. Morgan Cleveland School of Science after him.

The Golden Age of Radio

Radio grew dramatically in its early years in Cleveland, brought popular entertainment into Cleveland living rooms and changed the physical shape of downtown Cleveland. The first radio broadcast was made in 1906, and by 1922, *Variety* magazine claimed that there were 1 million radios in America. Cleveland participated wholeheartedly in the new medium. Large radio towers were built in a cluster near the edge of downtown on the Lake Erie shore. The towers were near the Ninth Street pier. This part of the lakeshore was being used as part of the town dump. A portion of the debris was cleared away to make way for the foundations of the several tall towers that would pop up in the next decade. The view where Ninth Street terminated into the large steamship pier was soon dominated by the frail-looking, ungainly, newfangled means of emanating mysterious radio waves. These electrical waves, of course, provided music and news right into living rooms of every Clevelander who owned a radio. Families would sit around the radio in the evening and listen to their favorite shows. More importantly, they would listen to the commercials of national and local brands and stores.

Cleveland's first radio station was WHK, which went on the air in 1922. Later that same year, WJAX went on the air, followed the next year by WTAM. By 1930, WJAY and WGAR were on the air also. To pull listeners in, local radio stations broadcast from venues all around downtown. The remote broadcast sites included the Rainbow Room at the Hotel Winton, the Hotel Cleveland, the State Theater, the Bamboo Gardens and the Hotel Statler. The 1924 Republican National Convention was held in the new Public Auditorium downtown. WTAM covered the conference and was the first radio station to broadcast coverage of a national political convention. The powerful signal of WTAM would soon allow the station to gain national prominence.

Radio revolutionized advertising in a way that would change the shopping habits of Cleveland citizens and the purpose of going downtown. Downtown soon became a retail destination. Euclid Avenue would benefit from the abilities of radio commercials to funnel shoppers to its fancy arcades and stores. Brands became nationalized. The old method of just painting a large sign on the side of a building or running an ad in the paper would soon fade as radio flexed its advertising muscles. Ironically, radio stations would run full-page ads in the local newspapers to ensure listenership. Radio shows all had specific sponsors or commercials that allowed companies to advertise across the nation for the first time. The citizens of Cleveland were bombarded with songs and jingles to convince them of the important need to buy these goods. With the appearance of ready-to-wear clothing, stores were able to stock national brands advertised on the radio. Brand loyalty would at times be tied to the loyalty of the listeners to the most popular shows. The local stations soon became affiliates for the larger national radio companies. WGAR became a NBC affiliate, and WHK became a CBS affiliate. This improved the entertainment content and created an increase in advertising income. By 1930, most of the other stations had also joined the major networks. The age of consumerism was born, and this also affected the urban landscape in Cleveland dramatically.

Cleveland native Leo Mintz played a pivotal role in the radio and record industry. Mintz had a record store in Cleveland, Rendezvous Records on

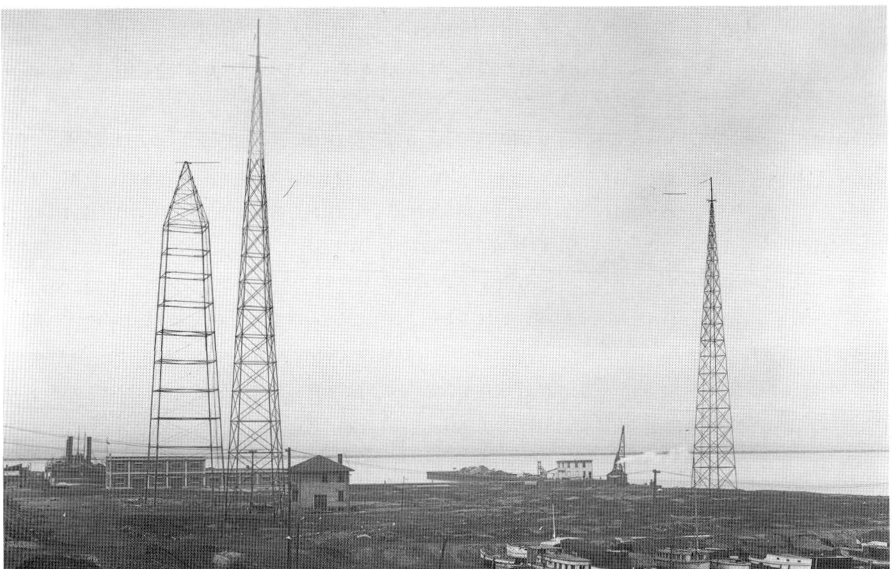

Broadcast radio towers viewed from the Lake Erie shoreline. The towers sit at the terminus of Ninth Avenue and the steamship pier. *Schwartz.*

Prospect Avenue. His store occupied the area in between the predominantly black area of Cleveland and the white neighborhoods. He sold records to the black community that he obtained primarily from jukebox supply companies. Mintz's was among the first to place records alphabetically in boxes to allow customers to browse the music. He also installed listening booths in the store to allow previewing of new music. In about 1950, Mintz noticed a crossover effect to a white audience occurring with his rhythm and blues records. He then contacted local Cleveland DJ Alan Freed and convinced him to play some of the controversial music. Mintz became a sponsor of Freed's *Moondog* radio show. Mintz also sponsored the Moondog Coronation Ball in March 1952, which is considered the first rock-and-roll concert. Mintz's efforts put Cleveland on the map as an originator of popular rock-and-roll music. This helped considerably in getting the Rock and Roll Hall of Fame and Museum located on the lakefront in downtown Cleveland.

Rise of Consumerism

As women became somewhat more empowered with jobs and the right to vote, retailers sought to take advantage of this category of customer. This helped to create the age of consumerism. There was a proliferation of incredibly dense and thick mail-order catalogues that arrived regularly on the doorstep of every respectable home. National radio commercials espoused goods and home appliances that would ease the burden of the hardworking modern woman. In Cleveland, mail order was not the only way to purchase goods. Stores abounded downtown, and downtown was considered a shopping destination. Improvements in household appliances were abundant at the turn of the century. These newfangled devices would allow more free time for the housewife to pursue more desirable activities. Most of these advertisements were focused on steering shoppers toward the national chains and large department stores. Women were becoming purchasing powerhouses. Their influence on the market would change the face of shopping forever. The corner drugstore or grocery could not compete with this new onslaught of advertisements. National products were designed to appeal to a broader audience as opposed to just local traditions or standards. Consumers could be convinced via radio of all the things they needed to have. Sales became popular because they could be advertised in real time. Downtown Cleveland by 1925 was heavily populated with

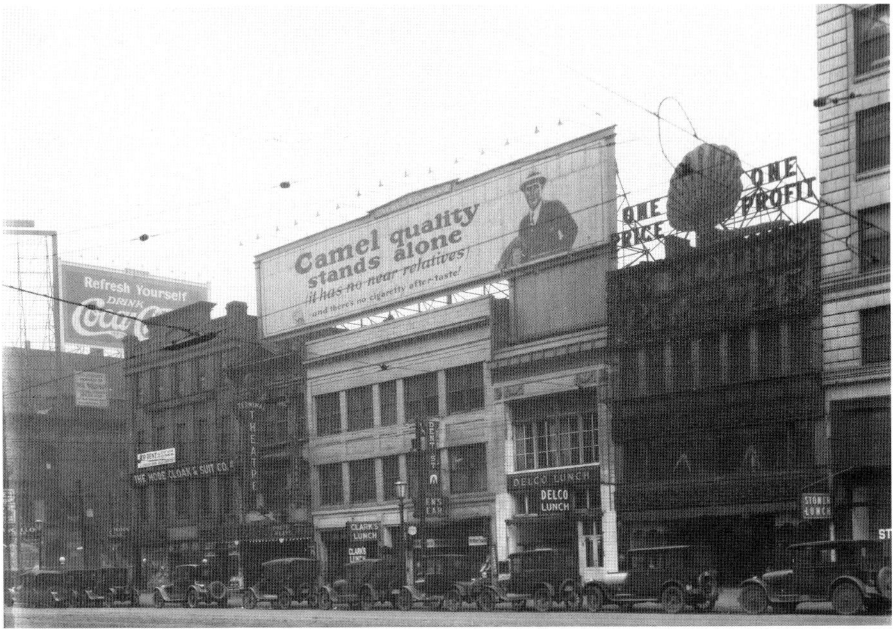

Superior Avenue between West Third Street and Public Square, circa 1925. *Schwartz.*

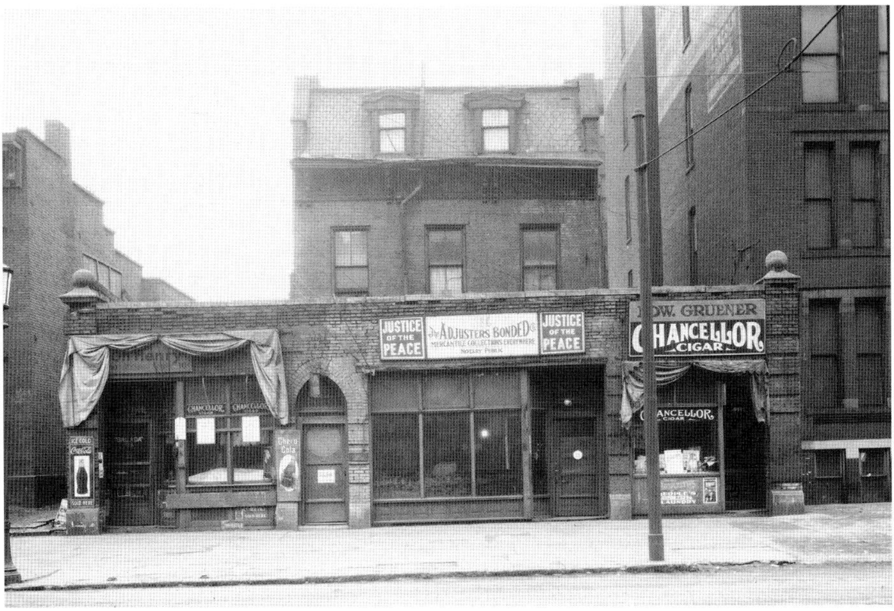

Various shops circa 1925, providing Chero Cola, cigars and hand laundry and notary services to the visitors of the new courthouse on Lakeside Avenue. These fine establishments were located at 1238 Ontario Street. *Schwartz.*

small cigar stores, barbershops, clothing stores and mercantile shops, many of them were in old worn-down buildings of Victorian vintage. The new modern shopper, propelled by the booming economy, wanted sophisticated stores with employees knowledgeable about all the new home appliances, radios and off-the-rack ready-to-wear clothes.

Not all the small downtown shops succumbed to the wrecking ball. Many of their owners realized the change in buyers' habits and rose to glorious heights as they adapted to the new level of entertainment or exclusive shopping being demanded. Downtown Cleveland experienced a renaissance of retailers in the 1920s. Cleveland's shopping district rivaled those of New York and Chicago. Ornate "malls" and incredibly elaborate department stores such as Higbee's, the massive May Company, the elegant upscale Halle's and Sterling Lindner-Davis sprung up around and down the length of Euclid Avenue, which by 1927 had become an enticing, vibrant shopping experience for the blue collar and elite shopper alike. As Cleveland's commercial district began to push eastward along Euclid Avenue, families moved farther east also toward University Circle and the "Heights."

THE LOEWS MALL

The Loews Mall was an excellent example of the lure of a flashy theater marquee and the enticing fragrance of food in a combination entertainment, shopping and dining package all rolled into one city block. The Lowes Mall sat at 312 Euclid Avenue, a very desirable short walk from the bustling town center of Public Square. Compactly nestled into one neatly trimmed building, the Loews Mall contained the expansive Mills Restaurant, the famous Rosenblum's clothing store, the Wormser Hat Shop and a small theater. Mills Restaurant featured a large open main floor with an airy second-floor mezzanine that ran all the way around the main dining room. Mills could turn over hundreds of customers per hour. The Wormer Hat Shop belonged to a high-end hat store chain based in New York City. It opened on April 15, 1919. The hat shop was decorated floor to ceiling in gleaming white enamel tile. Merritt Davidson was the first store manager moving from Minneapolis to work in Cleveland. This block of various shops and venues would compete successfully with the large department stores well into the 1950s. These clusters of stores had lower overhead, being much smaller, and they had more flexibility in changing products or replacing a store entirely as tastes changed. The growth of the shopping district eastward down Euclid changed the structure of downtown, pulling people away from the lakefront and the Group Plan Mall.

MAX ROSENBLUM

Max Rosenblum (December 5, 1877–September 5, 1953) arrived in Cleveland when he was six and was an errand boy for a local clothing store. He eventually owned a popular clothing store at 321 Euclid Avenue. Rosenblum was an early adopter of ready-to-wear clothing and easy credit. He was a savvy promoter and enjoyed all types of sports. In 1917, he organized a softball team and later helped organize the Cleveland Amateur Baseball Association. He promoted amateur baseball, bowling, football, basketball and soccer. Rosenblum was creator and owner of

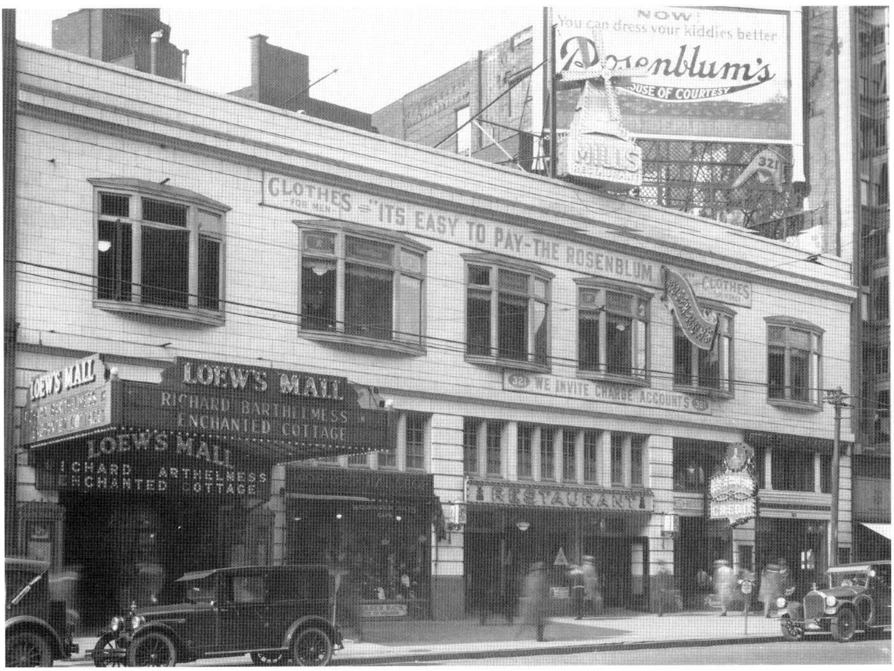

Loews Mall, 513 Euclid Avenue, home of the famous Rosenblum's clothing store. *Schwartz.*

the Cleveland Rosenblums basketball team—or, as they were commonly called, the "Rosies." Later, the team name would change to the Rosenblum Celtics. This was one of the first professional basketball teams in the United States. Seeing a need for a regional league to bring attention and order to professional basketball, Rosenblum hosted a meeting in April 1925 to form the American Basketball League at the Statler Hotel Cleveland. The Rosies dominated the league for a decade and won three American Basketball League Championships in 1925, 1929 and 1930. They played their home games in the Cleveland Public Auditorium near Public Square, averaging ten thousand people in attendance for the championship games. The games being held only a few blocks away from Rosenblum's store were an excellent advertising windfall.

With a quarter of the workforce depleted, the Great Depression reduced attendance to fewer than one thousand per game, and the Rosenblums folded in 1930. Rosenblum would go on to sponsor basketball tournaments held in Public Hall. Rosenblum's store was eventually torn down to make way for a large skyscraper.

A Cleveland Stalwart

The Clarendon Hotel, formally located on the northeast corner of St. Clair and Ontario Streets, was built in 1870. It was not a particularly grand hotel in the larger scheme of things in Cleveland, but it held its own among the many changes that occurred downtown and on Ontario Street. Ontario Street mirrored the many changes occurring downtown in the '20s and '30s. With its stone-trimmed brick façade, the Clarendon was the type of hotel a visiting aunt or family member would stay at if they couldn't afford one of the larger hotels downtown. The Clarendon in the 1920s shared Ontario Street with the Lincoln, Cortland and Rosen Hotels. Some of these hotels, such as the Courtland and the Rosen, were merely old Victorian homes that were converted into hotels and offered more of a boardinghouse service than a full-service hotel. The Clarendon offered an embedded barbershop, shoe store and restaurant/café to help with a homey feel.

The Clarendon managed to survive through thick and thin on the west side of downtown. It was described in different trade journals in 1918 as "Cleveland's most home-like hotel" and "completely remodeled, redecorated and refurnished. Everything new and first class." When this review was written, the hotel was owned by David Hawley and his wife, who purchased it in 1886. The original proprietor of the hotel was John Barr, an attorney. Barr was a local historian and the original secretary to the Cuyahoga County Historical Society, which later became the Western Reserve Historical Society. Hawley was a well-known Cleveland hotel man and had his hands at one time in the Weddell, Hawley House, City and Clinton Hotels in Cleveland. Hawley tended toward a hands-off approach to running a hotel and would lease the building for others to manage.

The hotel dodged many a bullet over the years as Ontario Street changed. One close call came when tenements on the north side of the hotel were to be torn down. The Clarendon shared a common wall with the sagging tenements. In 1930, the owner of the tenement block next to the Clarendon, Jacob Bassichis, wanted to clear out the block for development. David Hawley, still the owner of the Clarendon, won a halt to the demolition that would have left the Clarendon with the entire rear wall missing, exposing the back rooms to the outside. By the 1940s, the Clarendon was the only structure left from the original 1800s buildings erected between St. Clair and Lakeside. The hotel watched as many buildings rose and fell over the almost one hundred years the Clarendon stood on the corner of St. Clair and Ontario. The Clarendon managed to hang on well into the 1960s, when urban renewal finally saw it torn down. In its place now stands the Global Center for Health Innovation.

THE ORIGINAL ONTARIO STREET CHINATOWN

The east side of Ontario Street, in the heart of downtown, saw the site of the first Chinese immigrant community in Cleveland. This small community was formed at the turn of the twentieth century. Most of the early Chinese arrived in Cleveland after working to build the Western Pacific Railroad. Most of the Chinese immigrants lived in tenements that were sandwiched between the Lincoln Hotel on Hamilton Avenue and the Clarendon House Hotel on St. Clair Avenue. The Chinese population grew from 250 in 1920 to 700 in 1925. Surprisingly, there were fewer than 60 women among the men. Most of the growth of the Ontario Street enclave began humbly in the late 1800s. The Chinese Exclusion Acts, federal law since 1882, kept the Chinese population small and segregated. Chinese merchants, professionals and students could immigrate to the United States but could not become citizens. Only merchants could bring wives from China. The Chinese population did not exceed 100 until after the turn of the century. The overall Chinese presence was small when compared to the 800,000 people living in Cleveland at the time. The very small community on Ontario contained simple shops that bore the names Wah Chong Tie and Company, Quoung Mee Chong or Wing Wah Chong Crockery and lined the streets in front of and below the tenements. The brick tenements were three to four stories tall with chipped façades and some broken windows. The shops sold imported goods such as silks, teas, exotic spices, crockery and other imported items. There were also many laundry services and Chinese restaurants sprinkled about downtown.

Many of the more traditional Caucasian-owned stores around downtown would also offer à la cart "Chinese laundry" services. By the 1920s, the Chinese shop owners and workers were beginning to leave the small enclave and spread throughout the downtown. Most migrated east to the area near the corner of Rockwell Avenue and Twenty-First Street. The life of the Chinese immigrants was characterized by long hard days for very little pay.

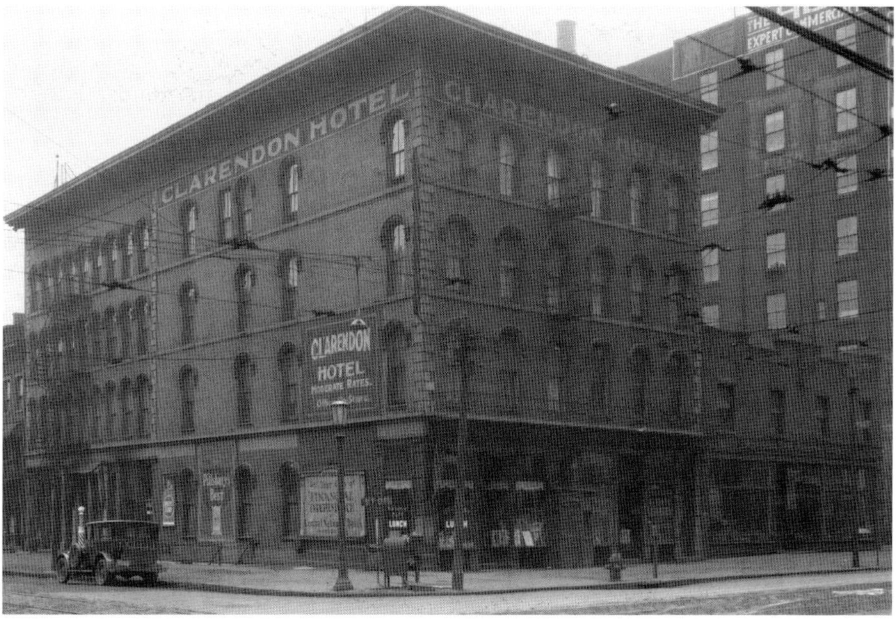

The Clarendon Hotel, at times called the Clarendon House, on the northeast corner of St. Clair Avenue and Ontario Street. Image circa 1925. *Schwartz.*

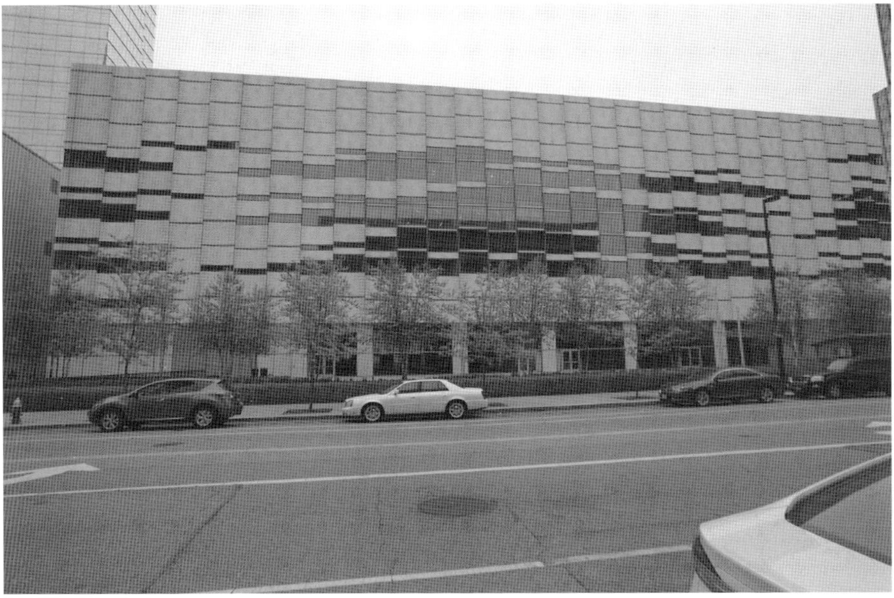

The Global Center for Health Innovations on the northeast corner of St. Clair Avenue. *Schwartz.*

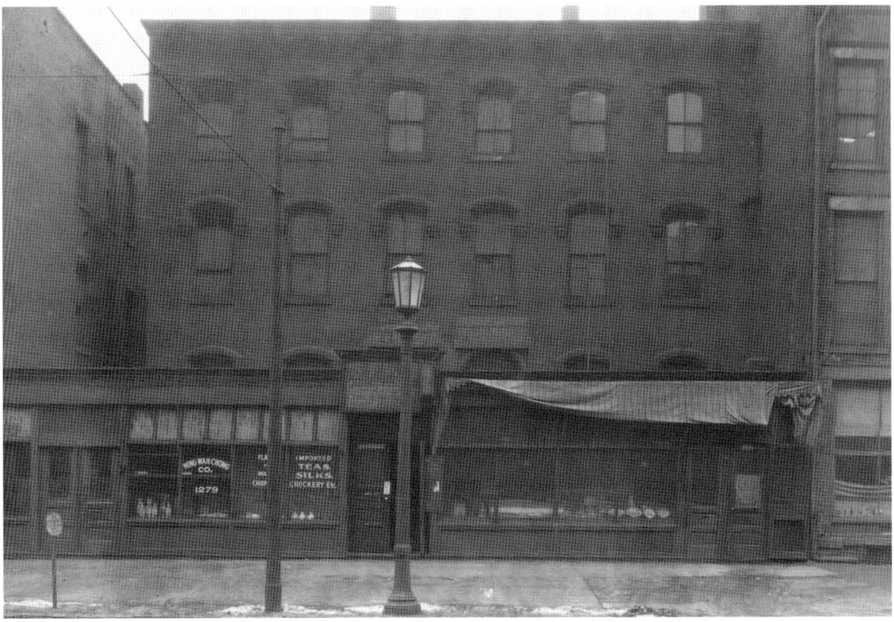

The first Cleveland Chinatown on 1283 Ontario Street between St. Clair and Hamilton Avenues. *Schwartz.*

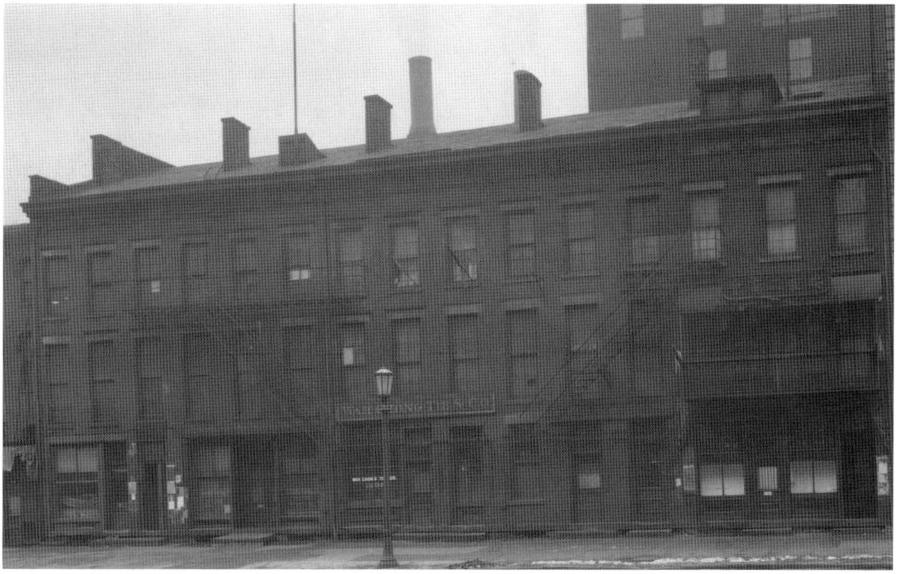

Chinese-owned businesses on 1297 Ontario Street between St. Clair and Hamilton Avenues. *Schwartz.*

The nearby Old Stone Church accommodated its neighbors by holding a Chinese Sunday school conducted by a Miss Trapp.

Chinese immigrants in America had many merchant societies known as tongs. These tongs were mostly originally formed on the West Coast, primarily in San Francisco's Chinatown. Cleveland had primarily two tongs: the Hip Sing tong and the On Leong tong. In Cleveland, On Leong formed in 1910, with Hip Sing forming in 1911. Some at the time referred to the tongs as "secret societies." These two tongs soon became violent rivals.

The Cleveland Tong Wars

The national convention of the On Leong tong was held in Cleveland in July 1924. William P. Lee, considered by some to be the mayor of Chicago's Chinatown, spotted in downtown Cleveland what he felt were "boo how doy" (or paid soldiers) of the rival Hip Sing tong. Lee sensed that there would be trouble during the meeting and asked Cleveland Safety Director Edwin Barry to provide police protection. Lee, who was born and raised in America, was at one time a correspondent for the *Chicago Daily News*. Barry heeded Lee's warning and apprehended any so-called suspicious characters Lee pointed out. Lee made many accusations against various rival tong members. The accused would be tried for extortion, bribery and kidnapping. Word of these arrests and accusations spread quickly, and as the men went to trial, violence spread across the nation's Chinatowns. Reprisals and killings swept across the United States, mainly concentrated in metropolitan Chinatowns. Fifteen Chinese men were killed in six weeks. On September 20, 1925, in Cleveland, the Bamboo Garden was suspiciously burned to the ground. On September 22, 1925, Yee Chock was murdered in a grisly beheading on Ontario Street.

When this violence hit Cleveland's streets, Barry had the police department raid all the Chinese shops and stores in town and attempted to arrest every Chinese adult in the city—612 Chinese people were arrested and thrown in jail. The people of Cleveland were shocked to see the immigrants jailed wholesale. All four Cleveland newspapers condemned the arrests. There was an immediate demand from the Chinese government to release the prisoners. The stores and tenements were ransacked and found to be bleak, dreary places, as opposed to the mysterious Oriental dens that were anticipated by many. Barry at this point also wanted to condemn and raze the Ontario street buildings. He did not get his way, but the old original Ontario Street Chinatown was torn down in 1929 to make way for a post office; currently, a sleek modern office building occupies the block.

The Chinese community continued to grow after World War II and migrated eastward toward Twenty-First Street near Rockwell Avenue. The tongs' power faded over the years as the immigrants blended into society and became more financially independent. The Chinese Exclusion Acts were rescinded in 1963.

PROHIBITION

Prohibition came to Ohio in May 1919, six months before the rest of the country. Ohio was a dubious leader in the effort to ban alcohol consumption. The Volstead Act, approved by Congress on October 28, 1919, did not outlaw consuming alcohol but rather the transporting, manufacturing and selling of alcohol. The landscape of downtown Cleveland changed overnight as the bars closed. Of more than one thousand active bars before Prohibition, only fifty remained open in Cleveland after the Volstead Act was enforced. Four years after making booze illegal to sell, thirty thousand Clevelanders were selling alcohol. According to the *Plain Dealer*, "A shot of blended whiskey cost a dime. Beer was fifteen cents a quart and mixed drinks no more than a quarter."

Lake Erie's sixty-mile width of water proved no barrier to the flow of alcohol from Canada. During some of the colder winters, cars and trucks would drive across the lake to deliver illicit cargo. By the mid-1920s, Cleveland was caught in the middle of local "bootlegger wars" between two rival gangs. Generally, most of the inter-gang violence occurred in the Woodland Avenue area, approximately near 110th Street. Despite Prohibition, business and industry boomed in Cleveland.

The Twenty-First Amendment was finally ratified in 1933, thereby repealing the Eighteenth Amendment thirteen years, ten months and nineteen days after its creation, bringing an end to the era of national prohibition of alcohol in America. At 5:32 p.m. EST, Utah became the thirty-sixth state to ratify the amendment, achieving the three-fourths majority of states' approval. Pennsylvania and Ohio had ratified it earlier in the day. Fortunately, no one spontaneously combusted due to being full of alcohol, as some early temperance supporters claimed would happen.

Eliot Ness

Eliot Ness, the famous gangster-fighting Prohibition agent, actually contributed quite a bit to the makeup of downtown Cleveland in the 1930s. Ness had built a national reputation as a squeaky-clean crime fighter in his days in Chicago. In that city, he built his special team of "Untouchables" to combat Al Capone and other infamous gangsters. Ness rose to the level of chief investigator of the Prohibition Bureau for Chicago. With Prohibition over in 1933, Ness was assigned to Ohio in 1934. He was the alcohol tax agent in the "Moonshine Mountains" of southern Ohio, Kentucky and Tennessee, and later in 1934, he was transferred to Cleveland.

The "Untouchable" designation referred to an inability to bribe his handpicked men. This was exactly what the mayor of Cleveland, Harold Burton, wanted in order to clean up his town's tarnished police department image. Corruption, fueled by bootleg dollars, spread among the police in big cities and was well known in the 1920s. Cleveland was considered to be one of the most corrupt cities in the United States. In December 1935, Burton hired the thirty-three-year-old Ness as the city's safety director. He had a mandate to clean up the city police department and modernize the

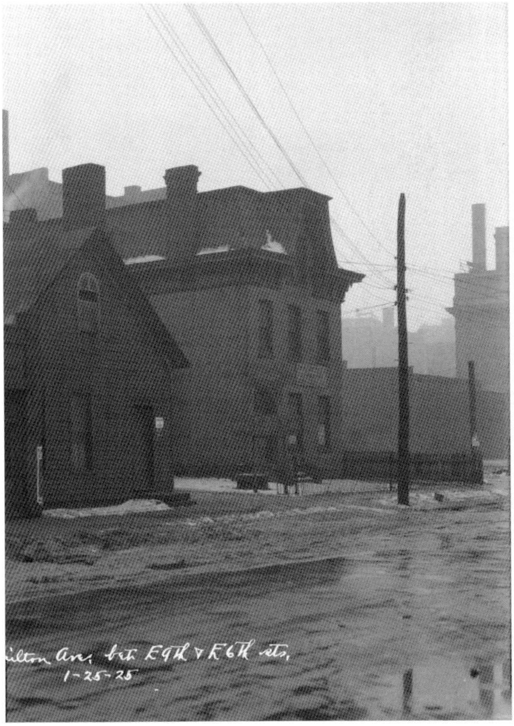

Left: The Central Athletic Club on Hamilton Avenue between Sixth and Ninth Streets. Despite the availability of boxing facilities, the interior was actually a speakeasy. *Schwartz*.

Below: Wohl's Hungarian Restaurant nestled between a garage and an apartment building at 1280 West Third Street. This building still stands on Ontario Street. *Schwartz*.

Opposite: The Standard Bank Building on the southwest corner of Ontario Street and St. Clair Avenue. *Schwartz*.

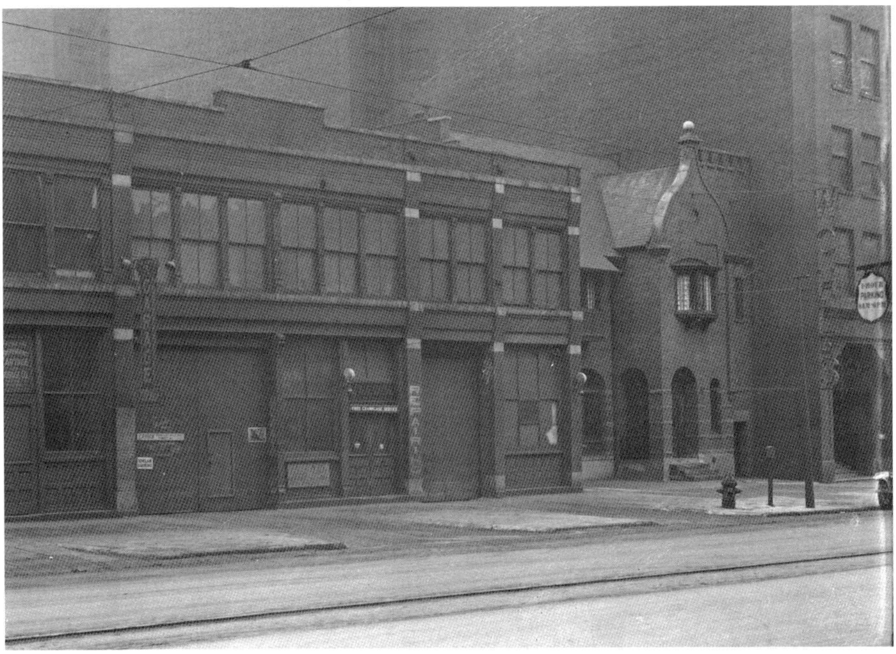

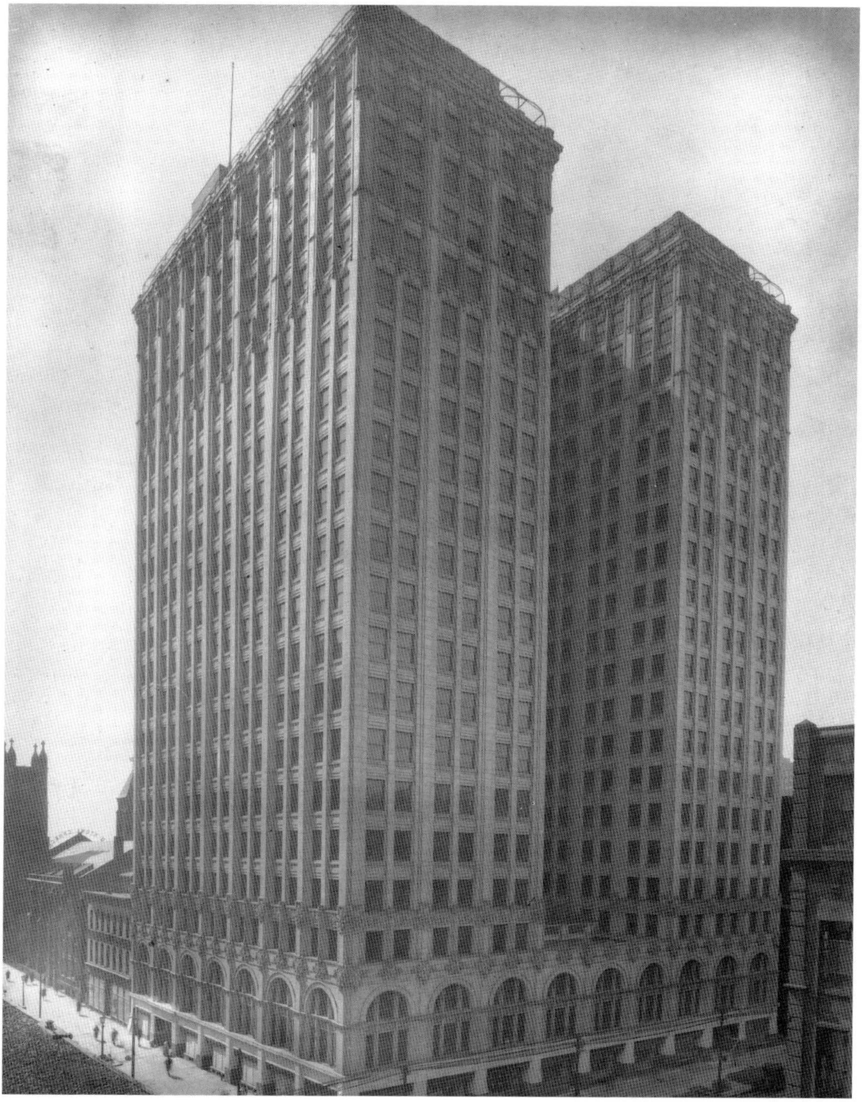

fire department. Ness immediately set about thinning out the corrupt police. He handed out several indictments within the police department, many of which were to people in high positions. Ness created the "Secret Six," Cleveland's own Untouchables, of which only he and the mayor knew the identities. Ness also defined the hiring practices of the police department to create a more professional level of new recruits. Prior to Ness, no Cleveland policeman had undergone a background check. During Ness's first eighteen months, crime dropped 25 percent, and juvenile crime dropped 80 percent.

One of Ness's contributions to downtown Cleveland was to introduce modern traffic control. This effort cut traffic accidents in half. Due to Ness's efforts, Cleveland earned the 1939 Safest City Award, given by the National Safety Council.

Despite his squeaky-clean reputation, Ness was not a homebody. He enjoyed dining and dancing and liked to frequent Wohl's Hungarian Restaurant on West Third Street. Wohl's restaurant was tightly sandwiched between two buildings near Public Square. The restaurant, with its unique architecture, appears to disappear or blend into the tall building just north of it. The building is deceptively large due to its very deep footprint in the block. Wohl's was a very popular eatery, offering entertainment and, at times, elaborate shows. *The Merry Widow* and *Madam Butterfly* both debuted in Cleveland at Wohl's. Wohl's started losing customers during the Depression and closed before the era concluded. The building still stands in excellent condition on West Third Street near the courthouse. Ness also frequented the massive Hotel Cleveland on Public Square. He and his wife, Evaline, frequently danced in the hotel's famous Bronze Room. He would also use the hotel for business. He would use rooms in the hotel for holding important meetings and for questioning suspects, including during the famous Torso Murders. Another haunt of Ness's was the health club in the Standard Building. Ness liked to socialize and play badminton on its courts. He managed to survive a political change of mayors when Frank Lausche took over for Burton.

During Ness's tenure, there were some high-profile criminal cases. The Torso Murders case, which occurred in Cleveland from 1935 to 1938, was probably the most famous. The fact that the Torso killer was not found started the decline of Ness's popular image. After a late-night traffic accident involving Ness (which he apparently tried to cover up), his popularity dropped to an all-time low. Without the favor and protection of Mayor Burton, Ness turned in his resignation soon after the accident. Ness remained in Cleveland until 1942, and then he moved to Washington, D.C.

THE GREAT DEPRESSION

The Great Depression hit the Midwest hard. The industrial heartland, now known as the Rust Belt, had Cleveland at its heart. By 1933, roughly one-third of Cleveland's workers were unemployed. Associated Charities, the largest relief organization in Cleveland, was the first to notice the onset of the Depression. In October 1929, 712 families had received relief from Associated Charities, and by 1932, the number had risen to 26,000 families.

Signs of the Depression sprang up all around downtown Cleveland. A soup kitchen was set up in Public Square. Shantytowns or "Hoovervilles" appeared on the lakefront north of city hall and at the garbage dump east of the new municipal stadium.

Some of the most prominent landmarks of the downtown landscape in the 1920s and 1930s were the great bank buildings. Two of the most well-known banks in town, Standard Trust and Midland Bank, had closed by 1932. The Standard Trust Bank building was a towering 285 feet and was the second-tallest building in the city skyline when it was completed in 1925. Banks traditionally used massive, sturdy edifices to impart how safe an account holder's money was in their vaults. The banks would proclaim in large signs on their buildings' fronts the millions in deposits to reassure the depositor that their money had plenty of company. The reality was vastly different.

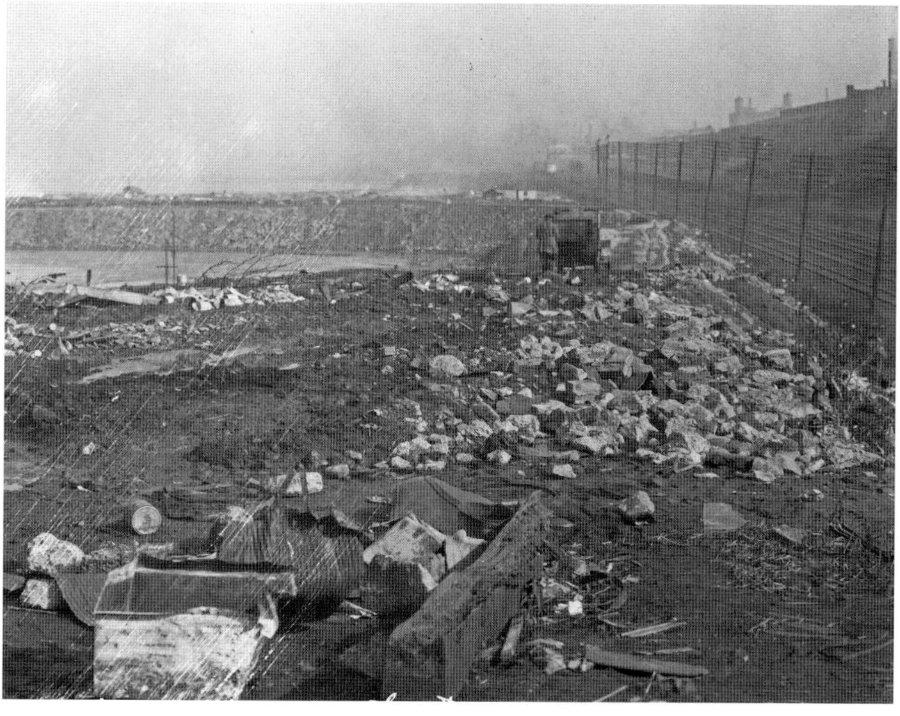

Trash dump along the riverfront downtown, circa 1925. *Schwartz.*

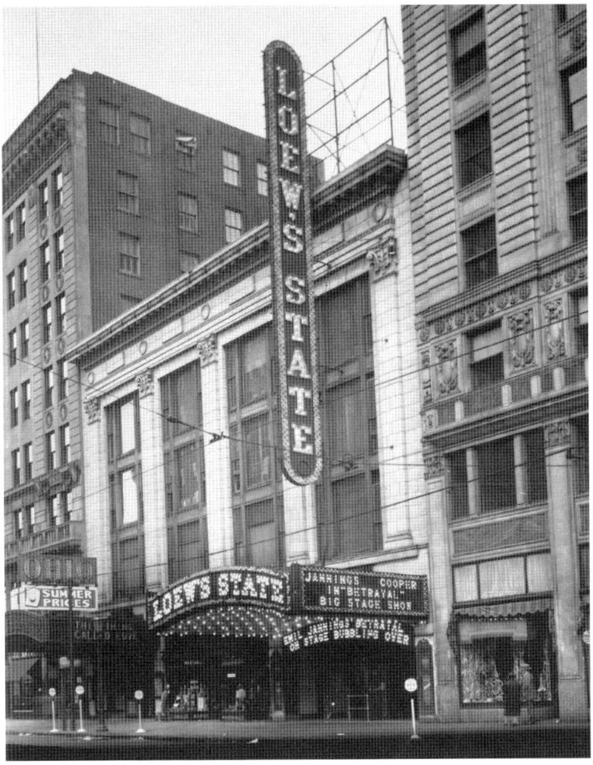

Left: Loews Theater marquee, Euclid Avenue, circa 1929. *Schwartz*.

Below: The Cleveland Trust Company building at 900 Euclid Avenue. Built in 1909, the building still stands today and houses a grocery store. *Schwartz*.

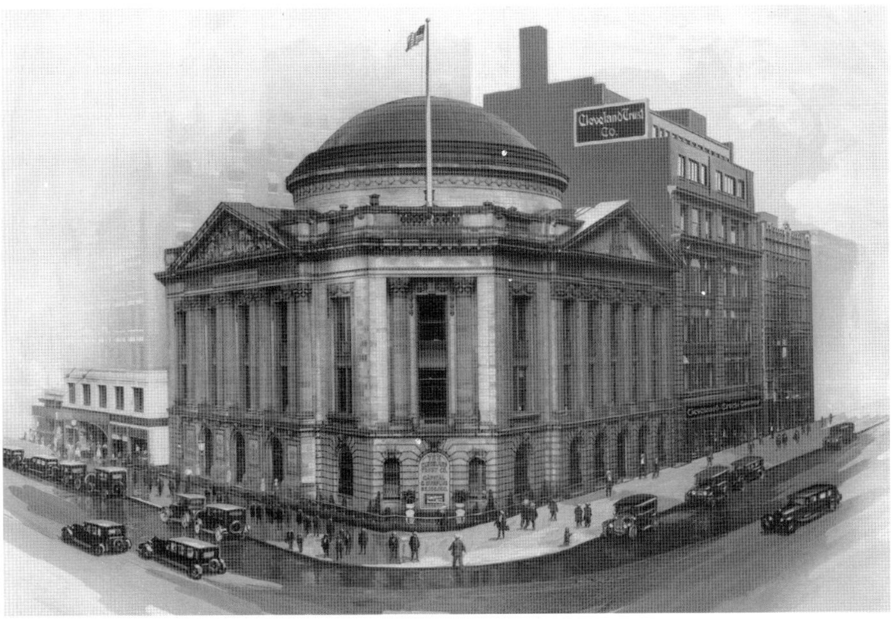

There was a run on Cleveland banks in February 1933. Union Trust, the largest bank outside New York City, and Guardian Trust lost half their deposits in the run. Cleveland Trust survived because its president stood in the bank lobby and promised depositors that the bank was sound. The Cleveland Trust building, built in 1907, was a visual anchor in the Euclid Avenue financial district, one that provided a sense of financial security to the shoppers and theatergoers who frequented the area. The Depression erased the public's faith in many of the big banks, as it brought these institutions to their knees financially. The downtown buildings would survive the Depression, but people's faith in banks would be shaken for a long time.

Some good came from the Depression in downtown Cleveland, such as in the form of the cleanup of the decrepit lakeshore. The Cleveland Memorial Shoreway was built by Works Progress Administration (WPA) workers in the 1930s. The WPA was created by the Roosevelt administration to provide jobs to the multitudes of unemployed. When completed, the Memorial Shoreway was a four-mile roadway from East Ninth Street to East Fifty-Fifth Street. This project also cleared out the shantytowns that were built on the lakeshore and removed the city dump from the same location. This new road would also facilitate access to the Great Lakes Exposition, to be held downtown in 1936–37.

Euclid Avenue

Across the years, Euclid Avenue has been one of the things Clevelanders always talk about or look on with fond memories. Over its nineteen-mile length, it connects some of Cleveland's best and most well-known aspects. In the 1918 trade paper the *Railway Journal*, it was noted that "Euclid Avenue is described as the most beautiful in the world. Among its other attractions is the memorial to President Garfield, a wealth of gardens and shade trees and beautiful residences." The downtown portion of Euclid Avenue perhaps has the most interesting history. The avenue has gone through many iterations, from residential to retail to commercial. In the mid-1800s, it hosted millionaires' homes and estates that rivaled the mansions in Newport, Rhode Island. Euclid Avenue was known around the world—*Baedeker's Travel Guides* called the elm-lined avenue the "Showplace of America" and designated it as a must-see for travelers from Europe. It then developed into the shopping destination of the region, followed by the addition of a great group of theaters to increase the reasons to go downtown.

Starting at Public Square, Euclid Avenue hosted several large department stores. Outlying communities were brought closer to Public Square by the efficient electric trolley system and the proliferation of the automobile. The stores towered over shoppers hustling between the vast arrays of colorful, enticing storefronts. During the holiday season, the storefronts attracted large crowds that admired the whimsical displays of holiday cheer. The concentration of shops rivaled what one would see on New York City's Fifth Avenue. Theaters appeared as the retail portion of the street solidified. The Playhouse Square theater district, as it is now called, was built by various investors from only 1920 to 1922 and contained the Ohio and State Theater complex, the Hanna Theater and the Palace Theater. Euclid Avenue was and still is home to the country's largest performing arts center outside New York City.

Of course, all these things did not exist at the same time. The large department stores rose to prominence downtown in the 1920s as the

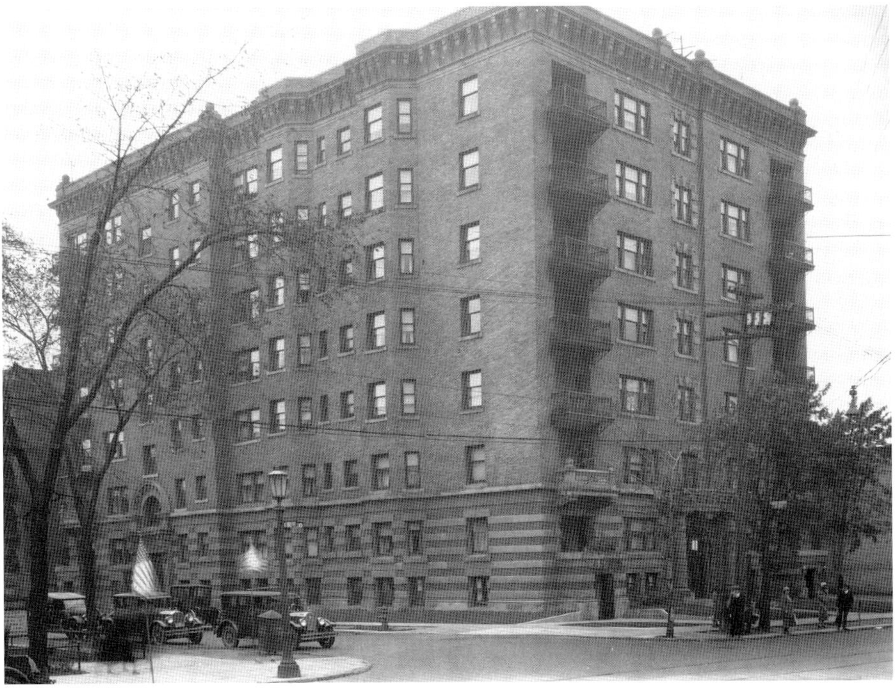

The St. Regis Apartments, circa 1930, at Eighty-Second Street and Euclid Avenue. *Schwartz.*

mansions were fading away. As Euclid Avenue developed and became more commercialized, the wealthy moved farther east to the more pristine "Heights." Many of the large homes were converted into multi-unit apartments or commercial office space. One was turned into a car lot. The dozens of mansions formally occupying Millionaires' Row were eventually torn down and are mostly gone—only eight remain today.

A microcosm of the evolution of Euclid Avenue is the Hotel St. Regis, located at Eighty-Second Street and Euclid Avenue. The hotel was designed by Edward E. Smith, a Cleveland architect noted for his apartment house designs. It was built in 1905 by the Euclid Genesee Realty Company. It was advertised as being a modern fireproof apartment hotel, containing 124 suites, with each suite having a kitchenette with iceless refrigeration and private bath. In its early years, it was the home of many prominent Clevelanders, including William Rockefeller, brother of John D. Rockefeller, and Frank DeHaas Robison, president of the Cleveland Spiders professional baseball team from 1889 to 1898. By 1920, Euclid Avenue had fallen out of favor among the rich, and the hotel rooms were converted into efficiency apartments. Even as an efficiency apartment building, Jayne Mansfield and Cleveland footballer Bob Waterfield lived there. They slept in pull-down Murphy beds and kept the hot plate on top of the refrigerator. By 1959, the building was being used as a retirement home. It was scheduled for demolition in the early 1990s and was finally torn down and replaced by a modern residential development.

The May Company, Higbees, Halle's, Sterling Lindner-Davis and several more large department stores offered Cleveland shoppers sophisticated goods and entertaining Christmas displays, and the restaurants in the stores became local favorites. The May Company boasted the largest store in the state. Sterling Lindner-Davis offered refined goods and impeccable service to its shoppers. Downtown Cleveland slowly shifted its focus from shopping and personal services to hosting office workers. The department stores pressed on through the Depression and managed to hang on until suburbanization made retail ghost towns out of most downtowns across the county. When the downtown office workers left for home after work, they were not inclined to return to the city center. Suburban malls, with their conveniences, won out over the large downtown stores with their glitz and glamor.

TERMINAL TOWER

The Van Sweringen brothers had the greatest impact on downtown Cleveland. Mantis and Oris Van Sweringen were inseparable brothers, born two years apart. Always seen publicly together, they were commonly known as "the Vans." They lived in a fifty-four-room mansion called Round Hill Manor, yet they shared the same bedroom, which was populated with two small canopied beds. They rode the speculative wave of the 1920s, buying stock that continuously rose in value during the 1920s. They added to their fortune acquiring several railroad properties by leveraging the value of their stocks. By 1928, they were worth $3 billion and controlled thirty thousand miles of railroad right-of-way. They were also highly in debt. Once they acquired a clear path from their residential development called Shaker Heights to Public Square downtown, they decided to build a railroad terminal downtown anchoring the two locations. This link would provide easy access to Shaker Heights and give their development a much-needed boost in house lot sales.

Their Union Terminal complex dominated the downtown skyline from the 1920s until the present. It would be decades until other buildings would be able to compete with Terminal Tower for dominance of the Cleveland skyline. Their decision to build the Terminal Tower complex on the south side of Public Square and move the main rail terminal access away from the lakefront affected the future evolution of the downtown from 1926 forward. Terminal Tower's 728-foot height focused the energy of downtown toward Public Square just at the time when the vision of the Group Plan and the Mall was coming together. Terminal Tower and the Union Terminal complex were so overwhelming in the downtown area that they could be considered an entity unto themselves. Downtown would then have two disparate competing viewpoints. The Mall focused toward the lakefront, and the tower focused on itself.

The Union Terminal complex's first phase would dramatically change the face of downtown Cleveland. About 1,400 buildings would be razed to clear the footprint for the massive structure and associated rail lines. Many of the small four-story low-rise buildings disappeared. The neighborhood on the southern side of downtown was erased. Even at night, the tower's presence was noted, with focused beams of light projected out from the forty-ninth floor. The beams could be seen from as far away as sixty miles on a clear night. The lights were used as an aid to navigation for airplanes and ships on Lake Erie.

By 1930, the Terminal building complex would be completed and would house a massive railroad terminal, large banks, Higbee's newest downtown store and restaurants and would be connected by a tunnel to the Hotel Cleveland. The new one-thousand-room Hotel Cleveland opened in 1918. The Cleveland would provide a natural physical symmetry to the Terminal complex, balancing the new Higbee's department store on the other side of the tower. The Van Sweringens purchased the Hotel Cleveland and completed one-third of the Union Terminal complex project with the stroke of a pen. The Van Sweringens spent $179 million on the complete complex and feeder rail lines.

The tower and terminal complex were built to last, but the Depression and stock market crash was not kind to the Van Sweringens' fortune. After the market crash in 1929, the Van Sweringens were $48 million in debt. Their rail empire began failing, and they had to sell off all their hard assets. Even though their Shaker Heights development flourished, their health failed as their money shrank. Mantis passed away in 1935, and Orvis followed one short year later. When Orvis died in 1936, the billions were gone, and he only had $3,000 left in his estate. The Union Terminal complex hung on as a train depot for a few more decades. The number of train passengers slowly dwindled as the automobile proliferated. The last intercity rail route moved back to the lakefront terminal from the Union Terminal complex in 1973.

Dragons of Change

Downtown Cleveland over the last century saw many of Tolkien's dragons of change fly by, and some even landed downtown. The changes were dramatic and surprising at times and sometimes subtle with little notice. Like most great cities, Cleveland learned that downtowns are earned over long periods of time. Cleveland's downtown has had many trials and tribulations, but in the end, the city has created a fine downtown with many different moving parts and interesting aspects and stories. The Playhouse Square area and downtown sporting venues all fell into place with older Group Plan buildings and the Mall. Even the Tower City complex has settled into a new role in redefining and helping pull together the new downtown identity.

A Vision Realized

Plans are of little importance, but planning is essential.
—Winston Churchill

Seeking a Connection

The visionaries behind the design of Cleveland's 1903 Group Plan had thought that an effective connection to the lakefront would be realized by a Union Terminal at the northern end of the plan's Great Mall. As discussed previously in this book, that vision was blocked by the opportunistic development of a Union Terminal at a different downtown location away from Cleveland's lakefront. This turnaround meant that Cleveland's connection to the vital center of its lakefront went unrealized—and it would remain so for the most part to the present day.

There were later visionaries who would promote various projects through the years to solve the "connection" problem, but unfortunately, each of these projects would be thwarted—some by war, some by politics, some by economic constraints and some by a lack of sufficient civic momentum. The only successful plan for a solution to the connection problem was realized by the organizers of the 1936–37 Great Lakes Exposition. The exposition's Court of the Presidents spanned the lakefront railway's twelve-track-wide expanse, but like the rest of the exposition's structures, the court's one-hundred-foot-wide causeway was hurriedly built and was only intended to

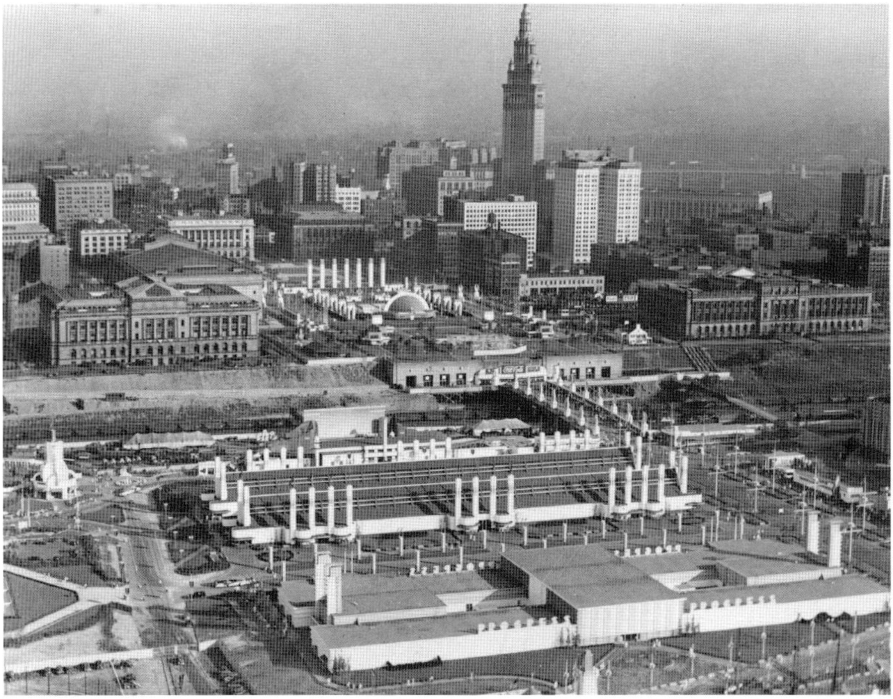

The Great Lakes Exposition's causeway (seen at center-right) provided a connection between the city's downtown and its lakefront. A never-realized post-Depression plan would have created a connecting plaza in its place. *Cleveland Memory Project.*

be a temporary construction; also like the exposition's other structures, the causeway was dismantled after the two-summer run, and it was tossed into Lake Erie to be used for landfill.

The exposition also had solved other problems. The development of Cleveland's critical lakefront properties that were adjacent to the Municipal Stadium and had become derelict city dumps and "Hoovervilles" were cleaned out by the exposition's development, and the need for a route for a lakeshore highway was made possible by a WPA bridge project that was created to provide a connection between the expo's western and eastern ends.

The exposition's causeway connector was the correct dimension to permanently solve the connection problem, and its configuration would have been able to accommodate vehicle and pedestrian traffic between Cleveland's Lakeside Avenue and the city's lakefront. It would have been relatively easy to dismantle the causeway and replace it with a more permanently built structure, but those who were working on the development of a permanent connection to the lakefront had more elaborate plans in mind—the complexity of their design plans would be their downfall, just as the elaborateness of the original Group Plan designs contributed to their not being fully realized.

A Second Axis

The 1941 Chamber of Commerce Plan for an extension of the Group Plan to the development of buildings along a second axis aligned with Municipal Stadium was challenged by problems from the start. The plans were adapted from plans for reviving the completion of the Group Plan that were drawn up in the last years of the Great Depression and were not seriously addressed during the post-Depression and war years. As mentioned, the plan's designs were too complicated to ever be realized. The designers had correctly

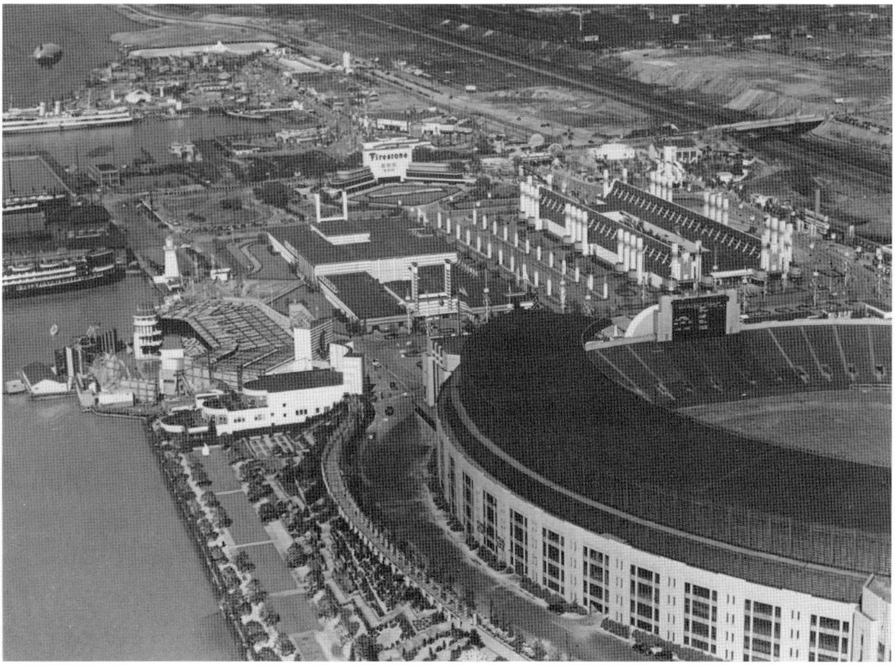

The chamber of commerce's plan would have created a second axis for the Group Plan, with a collection of civic buildings occupying the same footprint as did the Great Lakes Exposition's automotive buildings, seen here to the left of Municipal Stadium. *Cleveland Memory Project.*

determined that the accommodation of automobile and bus traffic meant that their design would need to include sloping causeways from the end of the Great Mall to the lakefront, fifty feet below.

The "connection" issue might have been accomplished by reconfiguring the exposition's Court of the Presidents causeway, but post-Depression plans for solving the "connection" problem were complex, with the problem being solved either by a too-large "cap" over the lakeshore railway lines or by a set of two curving causeways for vehicle traffic bracketing a central pedestrian causeway. These solutions required costly real estate acquisitions and complicated construction, making these projects expensive and time-consuming.

The Group Plan buildings for the project's northern edge, the county courthouse and the Cleveland City Hall, had been built; Public Hall and the Board of Education buildings had been constructed on the Mall's eastern edge; and the Main Cleveland Library buildings had been completed on the Mall's southern edge—all prior to the start of the Great Depression and before the wholesale shift of Cleveland's developmental focus from the Group Plan area to the Van Sweringen brothers' Terminal Tower project area. However, land acquisition that had been planned to allow for the construction of buildings along the Mall's western edge had not even begun due to poor economic conditions that persisted during and after the Depression. Cleveland's opportunity to bring the Group Plan project to fruition, and to solve its "connection" problem, had been lost for what would turn out to be a long time.

CHALLENGES TO THE VISION

Other factors were stacked against the success of development along Cleveland's lakefront in the late 1930s and early 1940s. The war in the Pacific had been raging since the early 1930s, and the war in Europe had been escalating since 1938. Tensions were high, and America's industrial cities were already focused on federal government contracts related to the production of lend-lease projects. Supporters of the Group Plan Expansion project raised public funds to explore the efficacy of the expansion project, but through the 1910s and 1920s, Cleveland's residents reflected their dissatisfaction with supporting civic development projects that weren't going to improve their financial, educational, social and neighborhood conditions by voting down a number of public referendums that would have funded further development of the Group Plan and plans for its expansion to the lakefront.

Despite the lack of support for expansion of the Group Plan to Cleveland's lakefront, limited vehicle transportation developments were made, including the construction of high-speed roadways to improve connections between Cleveland's east and west sides. The construction of Cleveland's expansive lakeshore high-speed highway alongside its existing lakeshore railway lines was done independent of thought being given to pedestrian access to Cleveland's lakefront, meaning that a solution to Cleveland's "connection" problem would have to be accomplished by an extraordinarily long pedestrian bridge—a structure for which a solution still does not exist.

Advances Light Up the City

In Cleveland, in the first decades of the twentieth century, increased population led to the incorporation of many cities, villages and townships. Cleveland devised an advanced system of building codes to reduce squalor in its urban neighborhoods. Medical advancements were being made in the city's hospitals. Public foundations, theaters, concert halls, performance centers and music settlements were built and established. Civic organizations were established to give a voice to varying political thought. Cleveland took part in establishing cutting-edge governmental structures, and a public park system was developed to give people a chance to connect with nature. The quality of life for urban residents was improved by the installation of electric lighting and the construction and development of public water supply and sanitation systems. Museums were established to give citizens places to reflect on their past. Modern roadways were constructed for the efficient movement of public transit systems and early automobiles. The city was recognized as an important civic location, and national conventions were held in the city. Telephone service was also established in the city.

The city's renewed hopes of acquiring the properties it needed to complete the Group Plan project, along with its period of uninterrupted advancement, came to a crashing halt in October 1929 when the stock market crashed, marking the start of the Great Depression. The Depression was accompanied by increased local political corruption and increased criminal

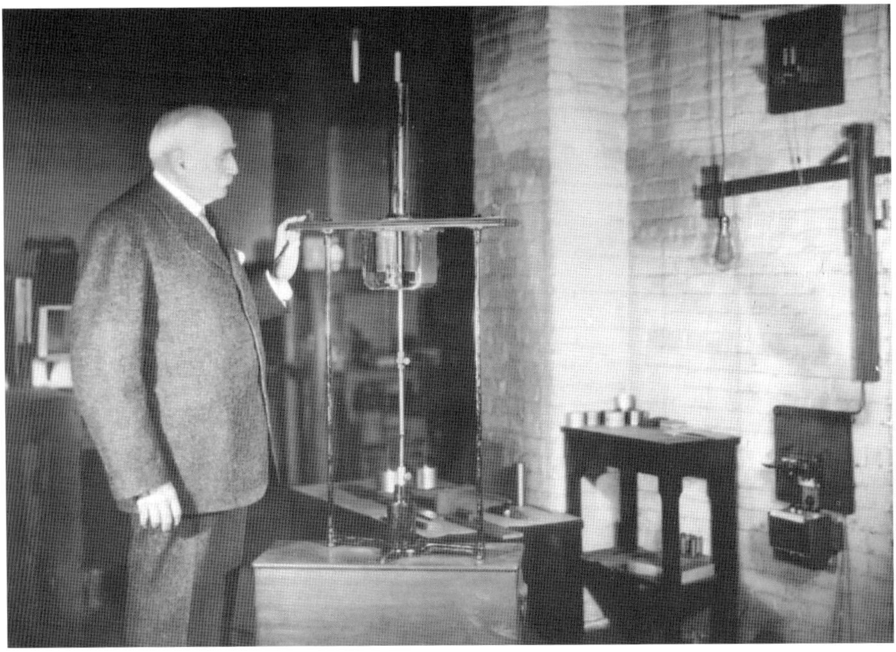

Clevelander Charles Francis Brush, inventor of the arc light, which was the first viable outdoor lighting fixture, in his laboratory at Cleveland's Case Institute of Technology. *Cleveland Memory Project.*

activity. Cleveland's police department was corrupt, and prostitution, illegal gambling and the production of illegal alcohol was ruling the city.

In 1940, Cleveland's population rose to nearly 900,000, and the city's post-Depression growth had just begun. Cleveland's industrial and technological successes had earned national attention, including recognition from the country's early efforts at establishing research centers to expand the nation's aviation industry. In 1941, the National Advisory Committee for Aeronautics (NACA), a forerunner of the National Aeronautics and Space Administration (NASA), was established at Cleveland's Municipal Airport. This development grew into today's John H. Glenn Research Center at Lewis Field. The establishment of NACA was an important step toward the development of the U.S. aerospace program. The committee's first projects included addressing and solving engine-cooling problems on the Super Fortress (B-29) and conducting research on aviation fuels and icing problems. NACA's Altitude Wind Tunnel, constructed in 1944, was the most advanced facility of its kind in the world and was used to test the nation's first jet engines.

In 1947, NACA renamed the facility Flight Propulsion Research Laboratory and then was renamed the Lewis Flight Propulsion Laboratory one year later. Over the next fifteen years, the laboratory carried out research in supersonic aerodynamics. In 1958, the facility became the NASA Lewis Research Center and played an active role in the development of NASA's Mercury and Apollo programs, including doing vital work on the development of the Apollo program's upper-stage launch vehicles that were used in the nation's mission to land a man on the moon. In 1999, the Lewis Research Center was renamed the NASA John H. Glenn Research Center at Lewis Field in honor of Ohio senator John H. Glenn, the first American astronaut to orbit Earth.

Ongoing Retooling and Change

Until its recent retooling and the establishment of a center for medical and technical research, Cleveland's health was always measured by the vitality of its industrial and manufacturing sectors, the most important of which were the manufacturing of iron and its products, as well as the city's ability to deliver those goods to the marketplace. Cleveland followed along the route of many cities that saw rapid development in the last half of the nineteenth century. The city prospered by becoming one of the nation's major industrial and manufacturing centers—largely brought about by its favorable location on the Great Lakes, which gave it ready access to raw materials that initially came into the city by water and rail and, later, by highways and airlines, as well as the means to deliver manufactured products that were produced in its factories and mills via those same transportation routes.

In its growth from a regionally focused agricultural center to a world-focused manufacturing center, Cleveland constantly retooled itself to meet the needs and challenges of the day. The city did that in the thirty years following the construction of the Ohio and Erie Canal in the 1830s by transforming from a city that focused on the manufacturing of household and farm goods for local and regional use into a city that could support foundries and manufacturing centers that could make iron into useful products, as well as large production mills that manufactured goods. This put the city in an advantageous spot by giving it the means to manufacture necessary industrial and commercial products to support the country's war effort in the 1860s, and the existence of the city's constantly evolving industrial plant

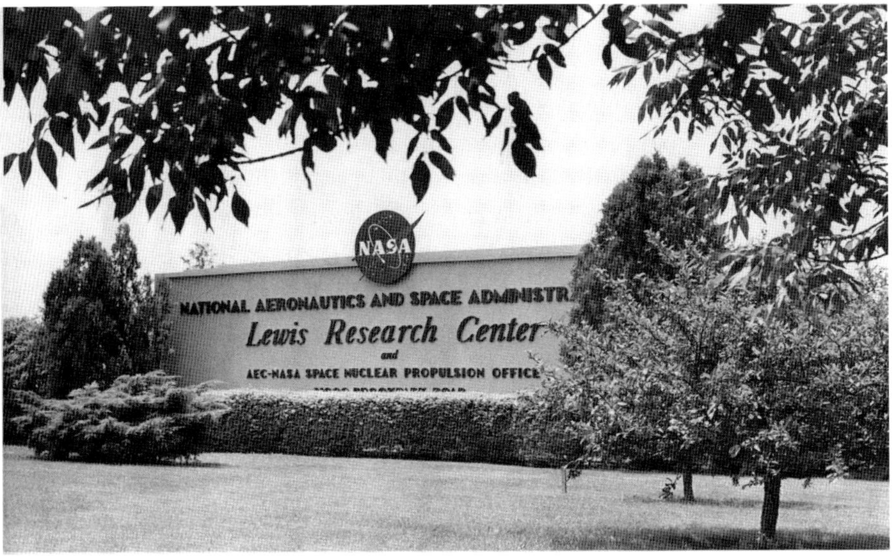

An entrance sign to the National Aeronautics and Space Administration's facility at Cleveland's Lewis Research Center near the Cleveland Hopkins Airport. *Cleveland Memory Project.*

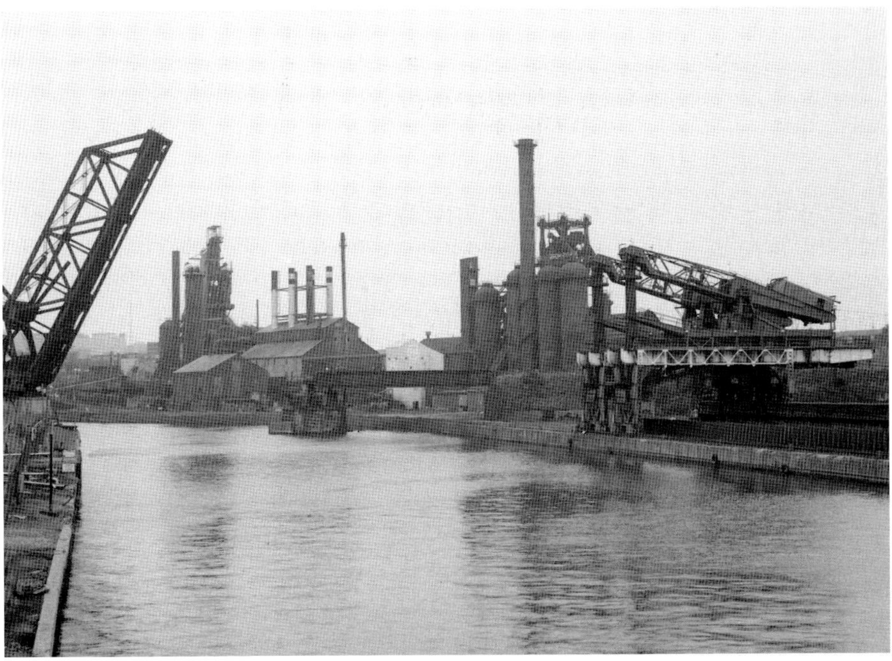

Steel mill on the bank of the Cuyahoga River. *Library of Congress Historic American Building Survey.*

allowed it to readily retool itself into a center for the production of goods of ever-increasing complexity, such as steam engines. Cleveland was also able to capitalize on its proximity to America's farmlands and become one of the nation's largest producer of grain products.

More retooling of Cleveland's industrial plant occurred in the late 1800s and early 1900s, as the city followed trends in production that occurred after the end of the Civil War as the country regrouped and its population expanded. In this period, the country gained an international footing and started to produce more products for a worldwide market. Because of its successful industrial history and its identity as a port city with access to raw materials and mineral resources, Cleveland was in a good position to capitalize on the shift of producing goods that depended on Bessemer steel and open-hearth steel manufacturing plants. In the early 1900s, Cleveland's primary steel producers joined the U.S. Steel Corporation family, and the manufacture of machinery and iron and steel products continued to grow. New products, such as Great Lakes steamers, and tools and machinery started to be manufactured in Cleveland, giving the city a new identity as a producer of top-level machinery and industrial goods.

Petroleum and Chemical Industries Make a Mark

Cleveland also benefited from its proximity to the creation of an entirely new industry when America's oil industry was begun after the drilling of the country's first successful oil well in northwestern Pennsylvania. Enterprising Cleveland-based businessmen, led by John D. Rockefeller, saw opportunities that the new industry could offer and quickly moved to gain control of the oil market. Cleveland once again retooled itself by creating oil refining facilities that were linked to America's railways, and in a short time, the city was able to become the center of America's oil refining industry. Rockefeller's pioneering efforts in dominating the country's refining and distribution of oil products led to the establishment of the Standard Oil Company of Ohio and the Standard Oil Trust.

In addition to being one of the country's leading industrial centers, the city was now becoming a major center for the production of chemical and petroleum products. This brought about the founding of many new corporations related to the production of chemical and oil-based products, including large paint and varnish companies, such as the Sherwin-Williams Company, founded in the 1870s by Henry Sherwin and Edward Williams, and the Glidden Company, founded by Francis H. Glidden. Sherwin-Williams would become successful pioneers in the production and sale of ready-mixed paint, and the Glidden Company would become successful in the production and sale of varnishes and enamels.

Further changes to Cleveland's industrial plant in the late 1800s came via capitalizing on the invention of electrical equipment. Clevelander Charles Brush became a pioneer in the creation of outdoor lighting systems with his invention and construction of an effective dynamo that could generate large amounts of electricity and an outdoor electrically powered arc-lighting system. Brush's system was first demonstrated in the late 1870s on Cleveland's Public Square and was quickly adopted by cities around the world. In the 1890s, Brush's company was absorbed into the General Electric Company, where his technology became an important piece of the production of viable electric-powered streetcar systems.

Around the turn of the century, Cleveland adapted its industrial plant to the production of early steam-, electric- and gasoline-powered automobiles. The city quickly became a major automobile production center, with the founding of three Cleveland-based companies: the Winton Motor Carriage Company, which produced gasoline-powered vehicles and has been credited with producing the first automobile for the open market; the Baker Motor Vehicle Company, which produced electric-powered cars; and the White Motor Company, which initially produced heavy, durable, steam-powered vehicles but later switched to the manufacturing of trucks for use in the commercial market. These three pioneering Cleveland-based automobile producers were joined by other automobile production companies. Most of Cleveland's automobile manufacturing companies specialized in the production of expensive, high-end automobiles, and when Henry Ford pioneered the use of assembly lines that could produce viable cars that were affordable by a larger number of Americans, Cleveland's automobile manufacturing sector collapsed. America's automobile manufacturing center shifted from Cleveland to Detroit, Michigan. Cleveland retooled its automobile manufacturing facilities into the production of automobile engines and parts, as well as into the production of parts and equipment to support the country's fledgling airplane industry.

At this time in its development, Cleveland was second to Detroit in the percentage of its workers who were employed in the industrial sector. While Cleveland appeared to be thriving, it continued to turn its back on its social

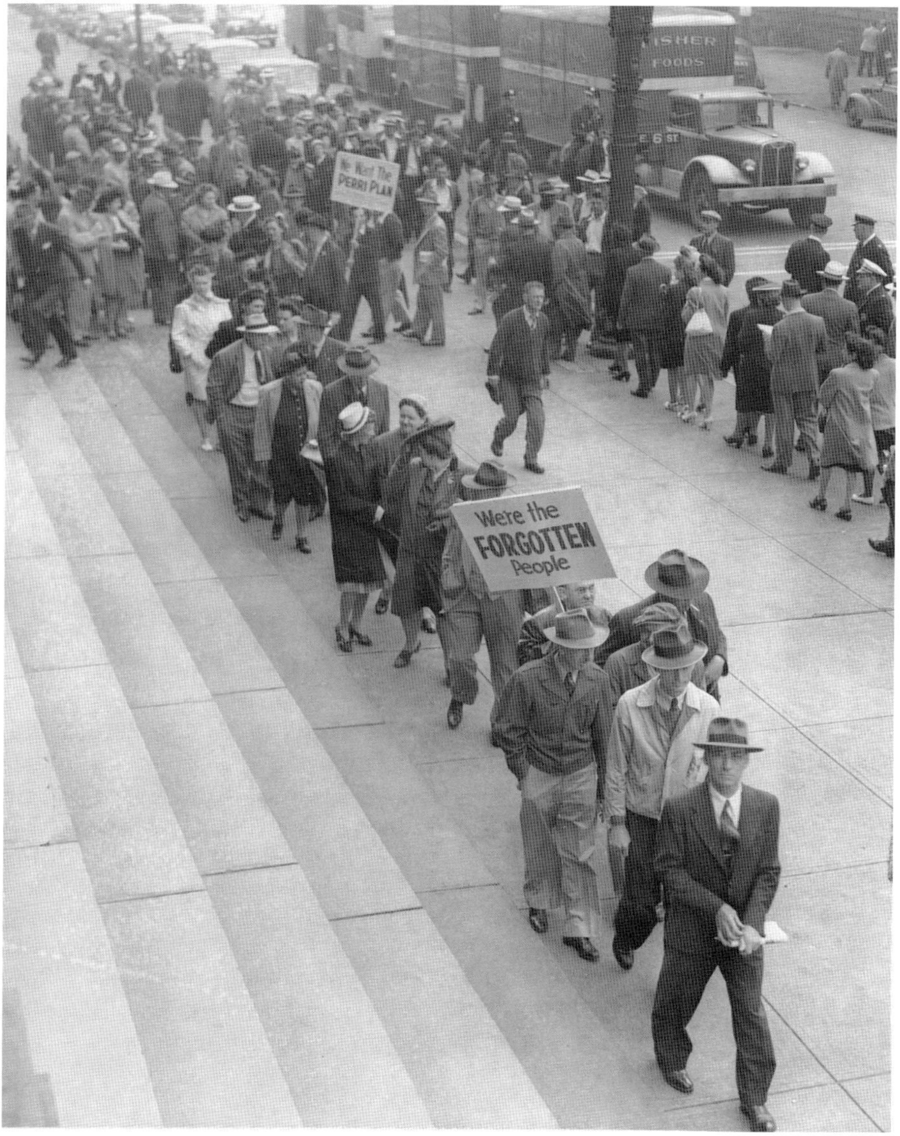

Demonstration by striking state, county and municipal employees on the steps of the Cleveland City Hall building. *Cleveland Memory Project.*

systems and on its downtown core. This resulted in increasing tensions between the city's more affluent and less affluent populations, between the city's industrial companies and its workers and between those who were focused on supporting and building its industrial framework and those who

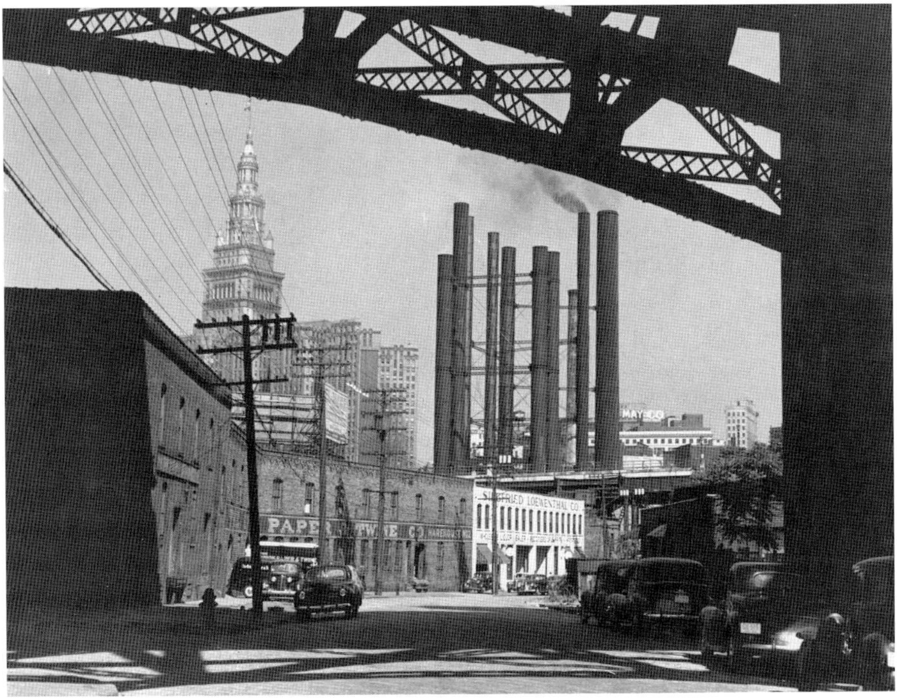

A street view in Cleveland's industrial flats section, adjacent to Cleveland's downtown area, showing smokestacks and the Terminal Tower. *Cleveland Memory Project.*

were concerned with improving the city's social fabric. These tensions led to a period of workers' strikes against Cleveland's industries and manufacturers that led to Cleveland becoming a center for the formation of strong trade and craft unions that gave a voice to workers and allowed them to negotiate for better working conditions and higher wages. These positive job-related changes brought more workers to Cleveland's manufacturers and further promoted Cleveland's industrial growth.

Effects of the Second World War

These positive changes to the city's employment sectors put it in a position to capitalize on the economic opportunities that accompanied the Second World War. While American lives were being lost in this war, including the lives of many Clevelanders, the city was able to expand its existing industrial plant and play its role in producing vital materials for the war effort. At the same time, many Clevelanders who had lost employment during the 1930s regained it. A total of more than 160,000 Clevelanders entered into service during World War II, and more than 4,000 of them lost their lives during the war. The city of Cleveland was economically and socially transformed by the war, but some of the changes that came to the city in response to its efforts to support the war would result in its decline following the war.

Clevelanders readily responded to the war's demands. They participated in blackout drills, they planted Victory Gardens and they tolerated commodity rationing programs that regulated their ability to purchase scarce common items such as sugar, meat, gasoline and tires. A large portion of the control of Cleveland's industrial plant was given over to government contracts that dictated what and how much was produced. During the war, Cleveland's Public Square and Cleveland's financial district (centered on the intersections of East Ninth Street and Euclid Avenue) were transformed by the addition of structures and offices that tracked wartime production goals, offered information and services to the public and served as public centers for the advertisement and sale of war bonds and stamps that were sold to finance the war.

In addition, Cleveland's Playhouse Square area became dominated by the Stage Door Canteen, which offered entertainment and hospitality to servicemen; the United Service Organization (USO); Red Cross operations; and offices of the War Housing Service, which supported the needs of Cleveland's servicemen and their families. Playhouse Square also became the home of the Telenews Theater, where in pre-television days Clevelanders could view continuous newsreels that provided them information on the progress of the war. In addition to giving hundreds of thousands of its citizens to serve during the war, Cleveland's residents were very active in doing their part on the homefront. Cleveland's wartime Block Plan program was formed to organize efforts to sell war bonds and promote blood donations and scrap metal drives, and it also organized programs for the collection of scrap metal in the city's neighborhoods and schools.

Federal Contracts Alter the City

The city's industrial base did its part to support the war effort and was expanded by federal government programs that supported the development of new facilities to produce needed military weapons and supplies. These facilities included the establishment of the Thompson Aircraft production plant in Cleveland's east side suburb of Euclid, Ohio, in 1941, which became the city's largest single employer by the end of the war. Two large production facilities were also established near Cleveland's Municipal Airport to produce tanks and aircraft parts. Also near the airport, the federal government built research facilities for the testing of aircraft engines, which eventually became Cleveland's NASA-run Lewis Research Center. Finally, a great number of Cleveland's manufacturing plants switched over from producing their normal products to the production of military parts. With the influx of funding from federal grants, some of Cleveland's workers' working conditions improved and wages increased during the war years. Employment increased throughout the city, with Cleveland being singled out for being one of the nation's most successful production centers during the war.

While the occurrence of labor strikes in Cleveland was greatly reduced, the city was not without its problems during the war. The expansion of the number of jobs drew many African Americans to Cleveland from southern states, resulting in a 75 percent increase in the city's African American population during the 1940s. Cleveland's infrastructure was stressed during the war years by very rapid population increases; the increased use of its roadways, rail systems and ports; and increased demands on its supply and disposal utilities. The availability of materials for housing construction was also an issue during the war. Cleveland's housing vacancy rate dropped to an all-time low near 0 percent during the war, and a large portion of the city's aging housing stock that had been neglected during the Depression years was further affected by the lack of maintenance in wartime due to restrictions on the sale and use of building materials.

Temporary wartime housing projects were built at a rapid pace but were unable to keep up with the housing demand, with many of Cleveland's citizens being unable to secure adequate housing. At the time, the city's civic leaders correctly predicted that the pattern of the degradation and abandonment of inner-city housing and its accompanying drop in tax revenues that persisted during the Depression and then continued during the war would set the stage for social conflict and a flight to the suburbs (away from the city and

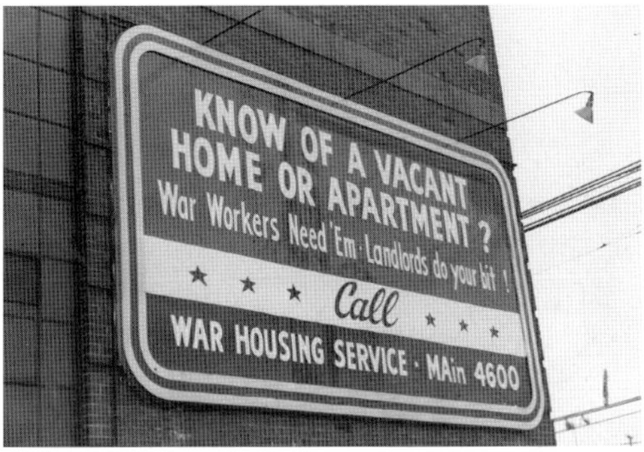

Cleveland housing was particularly scarce during World War II. This sign encourages Cleveland-area landlords to make their units available to wartime workers. *Cleveland Memory Project.*

its downtown) that would continue for generations after the war's end. The end of World War II was celebrated in Cleveland with a three-hour victory parade through downtown that was viewed by 300,000 people and was commemorated by the founding of a number of war memorials in the shape of statues and fountains in Cleveland's downtown mall and throughout the Greater Cleveland area, as well as by the establishment of institutions that honored the service and sacrifice of its citizens.

Many Cleveland-area industrial and technological firms excelled during the Second World War. These firms included Harshaw Chemical, Victoreen Instrument, Brush Beryllium and McGean Chemical—all of which earned recognition from the federal government for their contributions to the war effort. Several Cleveland firms also made important contributions to the Manhattan Project, which developed the atomic bomb. Much of the output of Cleveland's industrial producers during the Depression was directed to the production of machined goods under contract from federal government programs, and much of its production during the war was focused on the production of machine tools and weaponry that was also dependent on federal government contracts. The dependence on government contracts and the lack of control over fluctuating government grant cycles left some of Cleveland's businesses unable to respond to the production needs on which the city's citizens were dependent.

The city's dependence on federal support over an almost two-decade period of fiscal uncertainty not only affected Cleveland's businesses, but it also meant that the city's workforce suffered more compared to national averages. This inability of Cleveland's business community to respond to normal economic fluctuations continued into the postwar years and saw Cleveland less able to take advantage of the growth that took place in many of the nation's cities. The city had become stagnant, and its best years were behind it. It would take decades for the city to fully recover.

POSTWAR CLEVELAND

Cleveland remained dependent on its iron and steel base in the postwar years and gave little thought to retooling its economy to respond to new opportunities, although some effort was given to creating corporations that would become important contributors in the making of technical instruments, medical equipment, chemicals and plastics, as well as printing and publishing. Cleveland's efforts in cutting-edge research—in its universities and its research parks—resulted in advances in the city's industrial development and the creation of new technologies.

Photographs of Cleveland's downtown buildings taken from the 1920s through the 1950s are a testament to the environmental damage that was done to the region by its dependence on more than a century of a coal-powered industrial development. It would take decades after the Second World War for the city to begin to recover from a short-sighted industry-focused economic view that naturally brought about periods of severe downturn, high unemployment, disinvestment and social strife. Cleveland would go through a long period of stagnation until major investments would be made by new small manufacturing companies and the city's

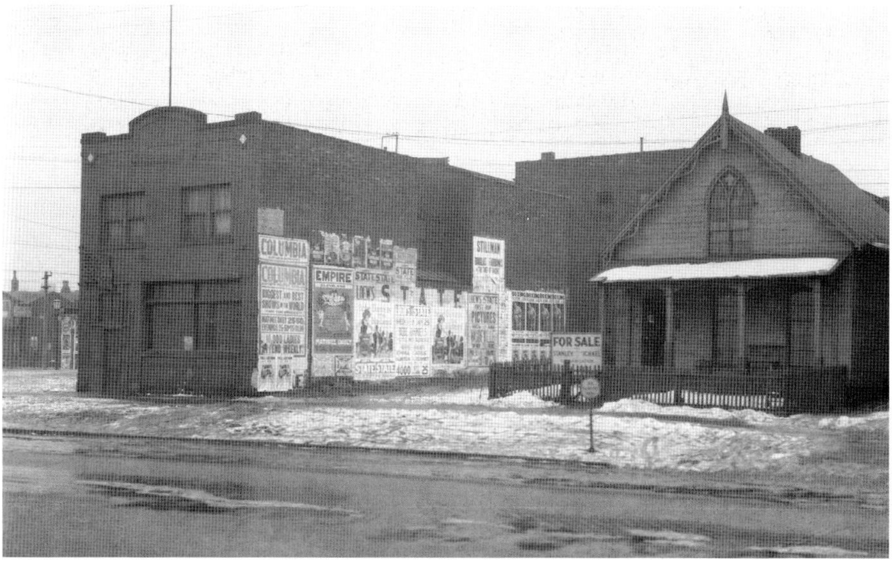

This mid-1920s view of nineteenth-century buildings, directly across Lakeside Avenue from Cleveland's city hall, shows the effects of years of the accumulation of industrial soot. *Schwartz.*

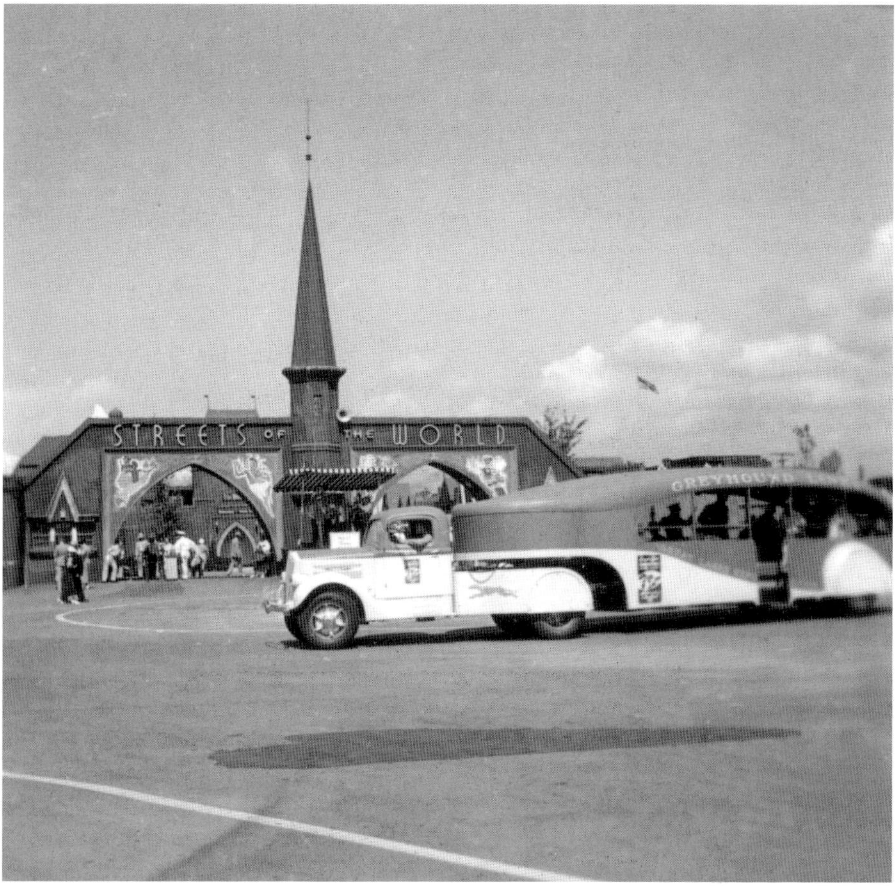

This mid-1930s vehicle was used at the Great Lakes Exposition in Cleveland, an early indication of the change from rail-dependent streetcars to free-roaming buses that would occur during the mid-1900s.

major employers such as the Ford Motor Company, General Motors and the LTV Steel Corporation.

During the postwar years, Cleveland was literally a city on the move. The construction of new automobile-centered roadways brought an end to the city's rail-centered streetcar and interurban train systems. By the 1940s, Cleveland, like most large American cities, had put major investments into building an extensive network of streetcar lines. Cleveland's streetcar lines were operated by the Cleveland Railway Corporation, which was formed in 1910. The Cleveland Railway built its system until the outbreak of World War II, when further development by the corporation was permanently stopped. In 1942, the Cleveland Transit System took over the operation of all streetcar, bus and trackless trolley lines, and after the war, the Cleveland Transit System undertook a program that replaced streetcar lines with trackless trolleys and buses by 1954.

CHANGES TO CLEVELAND'S RAIL SYSTEMS

Northeast Ohio's Lake Shore Electric Railway Company was a major interurban electric trolley that operated rail lines between Cleveland, Lorain, Sandusky, Norwalk, Fremont and Toledo, Ohio, and Detroit, Michigan. The interurban railway company was created from the consolidation of four interurban railways: the Lorain & Cleveland, the Sandusky, the Milan and the Norwalk Railway. The company's executive offices were located in Cleveland, with its general offices in Norwalk, Ohio, and its central operations depot located at the intersection of Bolivar and Erie Streets in Cleveland. In addition to providing rail service to Ohio's major north coast cities, the rail line offered excursion service to the Lake Erie islands ferry docks near Sandusky, Ohio, on the western Lake Erie shoreline, as well as to resorts all along the lake.

In 1907, the rail line operated 114 cars on nearly two hundred miles of track and annually carried more than 5 million passengers. One year later, the Lake Shore Electric Railway expanded its holdings by creating the Illuminating & Power Company that would generate electricity for its operations. By 1915, the rail line was operating eight daily limited stops that serviced Cleveland, Toledo and Detroit, as well as twenty other hourly interurban train lines between Cleveland and Toledo. The rail line's rapid expansion was short-lived, with the increasing popularity of the private automobile and buses taking over in the 1920s. The company continued to run a limited service until it ran its last car from Lorain to Cleveland in 1938.

BRIDGING TO THE FUTURE

In 1939, the city's Main Avenue Bridge was constructed to serve the city's ever-expanding automobile and bus traffic coming in and out of the city along Ohio Route 2. The 100-foot-tall, six-lane Main Avenue Bridge joins together Cleveland's East and West Shoreways, just west of downtown Cleveland in the city's Flats area, adjacent to the Cuyahoga River. At 8,000 feet in length, it remains the Ohio's longest elevated structure. The Main Avenue Bridge was preceded by an early float bridge that was co-owned by the villages of Cleveland and Ohio City. This bridge was replaced by a 200-foot hand-operated swing bridge in 1869. That bridge was rebuilt in 1885 and was converted into a steam-operated draw bridge. The Main Avenue Bridge took seventeen months to build and was jointly funded by Cuyahoga County and the federal government's Depression-era Public Works Administration of the Works Project Administration (WPA). At the time of its building, the 271-foot steel girders of its cantilever truss crossing over the lakefront's railway tracks were the longest span girders that had ever been built in the United States. The bridge was later rededicated in honor of former Cleveland mayor Harold H. Burton.

Other post-Depression and war years changes in the city of Cleveland included the permanent move of the Cleveland Indians professional baseball team from its home at League Park to the Cleveland Municipal Stadium. In 1939, the first nighttime baseball game was played at Cleveland's Municipal Stadium. The construction of Cleveland's Municipal Stadium on its lakefront was completed in 1931. When it was built, it was able to

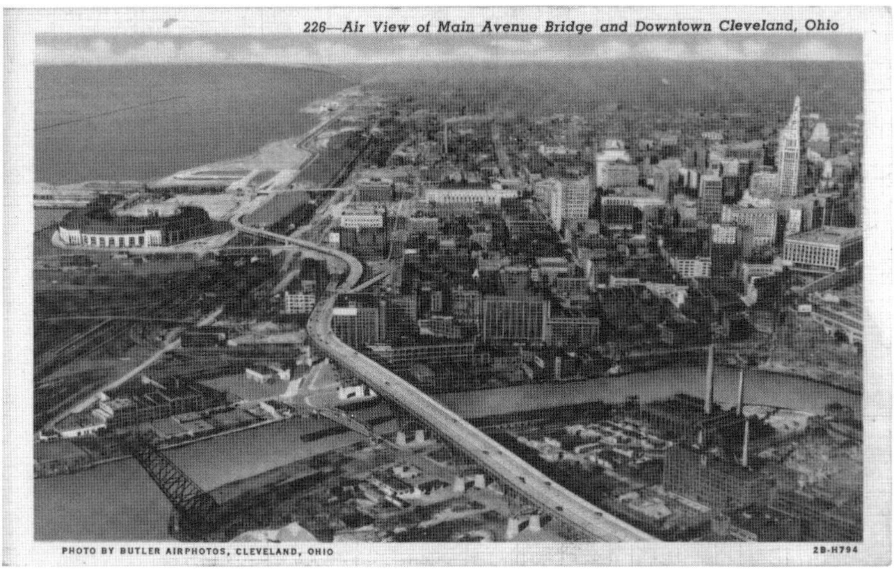

This postcard image shows the Main Avenue Bridge, which connected Cleveland's Lakefront Road on the east side of the Cuyahoga River with Bulkley Boulevard on the west side of the river. *Cleveland Memory Project.*

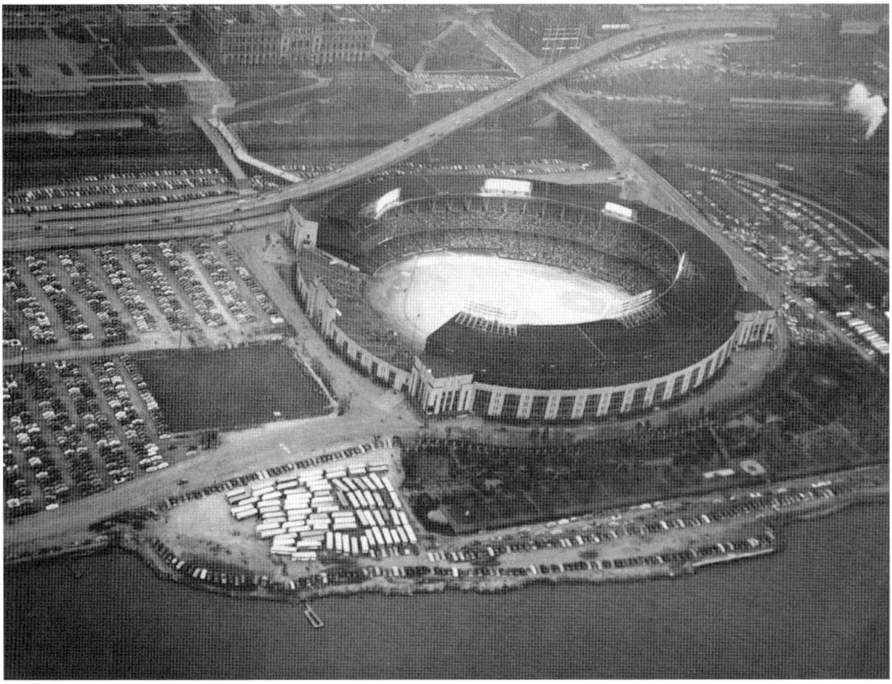

Aerial view of Cleveland's Municipal Stadium, taken from the Leisy blimp in 1950. When construction of the stadium was completed in 1932, it was the largest outdoor venue in the world, seating eighty-five thousand. *Cleveland Memory Project.*

seat more than seventy-eight thousand people, making it the world's largest outdoor arena.

The stadium's construction was funded by a $2.5 million bond issue that was put in front of voters in 1928. Two days after it opened, the stadium hosted a championship boxing match between Max Schmeling and Young Stribling. The Cleveland Indians baseball team played its first game in the stadium in 1932, but it continued to split its home games between Municipal Stadium and its traditional home at League Park. The team kept this schedule until 1947, when it made a permanent move to Municipal Stadium. That year also marked the Cleveland Browns' first year playing in the stadium.

The stadium has hosted a wide variety of events over the years, including concerts, operas, circuses, festivals and gatherings of many organizations. The stadium's all-time attendance record was set during the 1935 Eucharistic Congress, with 125,000 people attending. The stadium's heavy use led to its rapid aging. The stadium was refurbished in the 1960s and the 1970s, but its outmoded concrete-based construction continued to deteriorate. A little more than sixty years after it was constructed, the Cleveland Indians left the stadium for the city's new baseball stadium, Jacobs Field, which is located on land adjacent to Cleveland's Tower City project, which surrounds the Van Sweringens' Terminal Tower.

One year later, in 1995, the owner of the Cleveland Browns announced that he was going to move the Cleveland Browns football team to the city of Baltimore, Maryland. This announcement signaled the end for Municipal Stadium, and arrangements were made for the creation of a new Cleveland Browns team in the city a few years later—and with it the construction of a new football stadium, First Energy Field, which was built on land that was occupied by Municipal Stadium's parking area. A casualty of Municipal Stadium's demolition was the destruction of the last vestige of the Great Lakes Exposition, the last remaining part of the exposition's Horticultural Gardens, which had been renamed after its designer, Donald Gray.

Lasting Additions

A lasting addition to the city was the Cleveland Bomber Plant, which was constructed in 1942. The plant was constructed under a federal government defense grant to build the B-29 bomber and was operated by the General Motors Corporation as the Fisher Body Aircraft Plant No. 2. At its peak production, the plant employed fifteen thousand workers, many of whom lived in nearby housing projects. After the war ended, the plant went through a number of configurations and uses. In 1950, General Motors chose the plant for the site of its tank manufacturing plant. In its new life, the Cadillac Tank Plant employed six thousand workers. The plant suffered a setback in 1952 when tanks that were manufactured at the facility were rejected by the U.S. Army due to a gun mechanism problem. The problem was quickly solved, and the plant continued its production through 1955. Tanks and other armaments were constructed by the plant until 1972. The plant sat vacant until 1977, when it was converted into an international trade market. In 1985, the facility was renamed the I-X Center, and it became the world's largest single-building exhibition facility.

Cleveland's Cultural Gardens, a collection of ethnic gardens along the slopes of Cleveland's East Boulevard that stretched from University Circle to the lakefront, was dedicated in 1943. The gardens were founded in 1925 as the Civic Progress League by the Cleveland Cultural Garden Foundation,

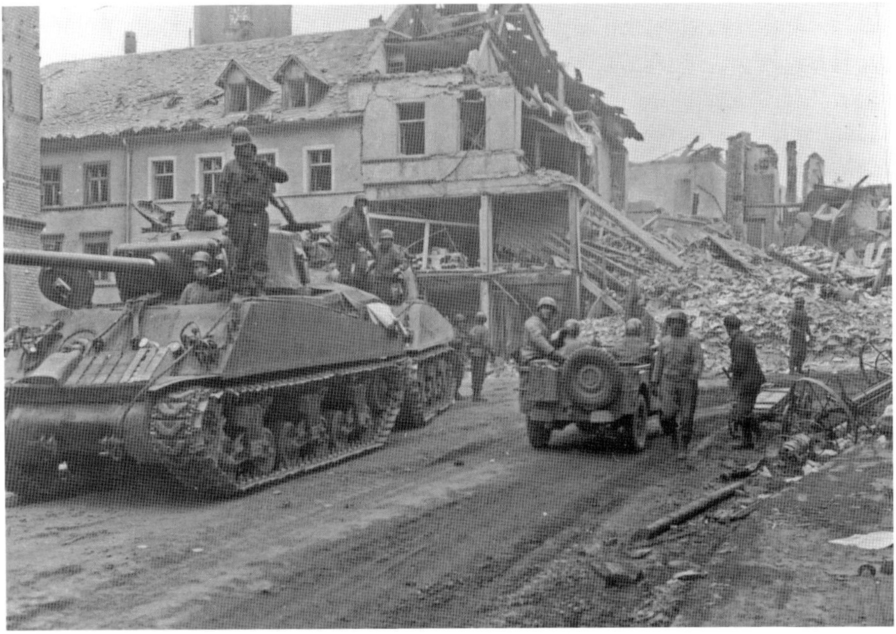

This Sherman tank, circa 1944, is an example of the type of armaments built at Cleveland's massive tank plant. The plant employed six thousand and manufactured wheeled armaments from the post–World War II years until the federal government's program ended in 1972. *Ford.*

which one year later became the Cultural Garden League. Over the following decade, ethnic gardens were created in Rockefeller Park to honor Cleveland's Italian, German, Lithuanian, Slovak, Ukrainian, Polish, Hungarian, Czech, Yugoslav, Rusin, Irish, Greek, Syrian, Romanian, Estonian, Afro-American, Chinese, Finnish and Indian communities. During the 1960s and 1970s, many of the park's gardens were vandalized, and statuary from the gardens was removed for safekeeping. In 1985, a major garden rehabilitation program was undertaken to restore the park's gardens.

Tragedy struck the city in 1944 when 130 people were killed by the explosion of two enormous natural liquid gas tanks at the city's East Ohio Gas facility. The explosion also caused the largest fire in the city's history, destroying a one-square-mile area of homes and businesses on Cleveland's east side. The fire spread through a twenty-block area and through the neighborhood's underground sewer system. Nearly 700 residents were left homeless by the explosion. The resulting fires destroyed seventy-nine homes and two factories.

The abandonment of Cleveland's downtown and its inner-city neighborhoods, foretold by its leaders during the Second World War, came about even faster than was predicted, as returning military veterans looked to take advantage of government-sponsored mortgages to build their American dream in Cleveland's suburbs and in lands far from Lake Erie's shores. Their flight to the suburbs was unwittingly made easier by the postwar construction of a national freeway system.

Following the end of World War II, many of Cleveland's industries were able to retool their production lines and turn over to manufacturing the types of domestic products that would be needed by America's families during the postwar baby boom, including homes, automobiles and home appliances. This trend continued in the postwar housing boom that saw tens of thousands of new homes constructed in suburban areas for new families who sought cleaner and greener neighborhoods away from the soot and smoke that was created by the ring of factories and mills around downtown Cleveland. These new suburban neighborhoods were outside the reach of the city's interurban rail lines and streetcar lines, but advancements were made in the production of automobiles and buses that gave suburb dwellers the means to access the goods they needed from newly developed and convenient shopping centers.

Unfortunately, most of the city's African American residents were left out of the newfound affluence that accompanied the creation of Cleveland's postwar boom and were left behind in the city's inner ring of steadily deteriorating neighborhoods. Again, the same problems that were seen in Cleveland and many of America's industrial-based cities during the twentieth century's first quarter—the inability of city leaders to recognize that they needed to include social and economic factors into their development plans—were being repeated and were again threatening the future of these cities' neighborhoods, downtowns and overall progress.

During its Depression years, Cleveland's downtown financial and shopping districts deteriorated due to the failures of individuals and businesses. They continued to deteriorate in the post-Depression years as the city struggled to recuperate. They rebounded somewhat during the war years as government-backed expansion programs were implemented, but they suffered yet again during the postwar years as many Clevelanders fled to newly developed suburbs. New suburban cities that were founded during the postwar years included Bedford, Berea, Euclid, Garfield Heights, Rocky River, Parma, Shaker Heights, Maple Heights, University Heights and South Euclid.

All was not doom and gloom for Cleveland in the postwar years, however. In 1947, Cleveland's Burke Lakefront Airport was opened just east of the area that was occupied by the Great Lakes Exposition, on land that was claimed by infilling a part of Lake Erie. In the same year, Dr. Claude Beck of the University Hospitals became the first person to successfully defibrillate a human heart. Commercial television broadcasting also came to Cleveland in 1947, and in 1948, the Cleveland Indians won the World Series. One year later, Cleveland was named an all-American city for the first time. Finally, in 1950, Cleveland reached its highest population, with nearly 915,000 residents, and the city was advertised as being the "Best Location in the Nation" by businessmen who recognized the city's potential for growth and change.

A Vision to the Future

The future depends on what you do today.
—Mahatma Gandhi

Cleveland is a restless city that has always had big ambitions. From the first glimmers of the Group Plan in 1903 until the present, its citizens have been creating plans to make the city a better place to live. It is not a city prone to remaining static, and it does not resist change. With heavy industry waning in the United States, this Rust Belt city has been busy trying to redefine itself. To move forward, it must have a vision that adjusts to the needs of its citizens and to the demands of industry. Efforts to adjust and improve are just as difficult and tumultuous in the present as the changes the city made at the turn of the prior century. The key to a successful future for Cleveland is in keeping its most valuable asset, people, in the city. In the last four decades, Cleveland has experienced an ebb and flow in the movement of its citizens. Mostly the direction of the flow of people has been away from the city.

The 1970s marked the low point of the city on many fronts. During that dark decade, Cleveland lost 23.6 percent of its population, far more than the national average. It became the first major American city since the Great Depression to default on its loans. Downtown, the theater district surrounding Playhouse Square was slated to become a parking lot. Urban renewal was turning many of the great buildings downtown into expansive parking lots. Brick and stone were giving way—without regard to their architectural significance—to asphalt at an alarming pace. Some neighborhoods benefited from urban renewal due to the level of poverty found in those areas, but the theme in downtown seemed to be to create parking space wherever there was a building in poor shape. Highways cut through neighborhoods, ripping apart the fabric of many solid communities. The Cuyahoga River had become famous for its 1969 fire, and Lake Erie was slowly dying. At some point, a city hits bottom. All these events in one way or another forced people to consider change in the city.

The transformation of Cleveland's downtown was not going to be quick. Over the years, committees were formed, surveys were conducted and collated and action has been taken. In recent years, the desire to revive downtown Cleveland in an interesting and livable way has taken on a life of its own. The results of all the information gathering has drawn interest in improving housing, shopping options, restaurants, more green space, transportation, cleanliness, new forward-looking jobs and safety. Unlike the original Group Plan, a holistic approach is being used to create a truly forward-looking and hopefully permanent process to the rejuvenation of downtown.

WHAT HAS HAPPENED IN THE RUST BELT?

With the impetus for change in the air, the industrial valley south of downtown had to be considered in any plans. Downtown Cleveland has always had an intimate relationship with its industrial base. Cleveland, like many great cities, has a river that runs through it. The Cuyahoga River facilitated the buildup of a mighty industrial valley, sometimes called the "Industrial Flats," to the immediate south and west of the downtown area. To the north were the docks of Lake Erie, with its access to international shipping. The movement of raw materials and goods was easy to facilitate through the river and lakefront docks. Add the major rail lines along the lakefront and Cleveland becomes a natural transportation portal between the East Coast and the heartland.

Initially, the citizens of Cleveland were tolerant of the industrial complex that sprang up around the river and its proximity to downtown. It meant jobs and wages first and foremost. The environment was not a consideration during the Industrial Revolution. As time wore on, the workers living downtown did not want to be near the belching smokestacks and the heavily fouled river. The factories were not moving, so the people did. The exodus out of downtown began. There was not a specific day to note that people started leaving—it was a gradual move over decades, facilitated by ever-improving modes of transportation.

The population of the downtown area has been boom and bust over the last one hundred years. People initially moved to downtown in the 1800s because that was where the jobs were. The steel mills and the auto industry ringing the city have always been the backbone of Cleveland's job market. Neighborhoods quickly sprang up around the large steel mills and chemical factories. Cleveland was well situated in the industrial crossroads of the United States. Cuyahoga County, in 1900, produced 968,801 tons of iron and steel, ranking the city fifth nationally in this category.

By the early 1970s, Cleveland's steelmakers were facing rampant inflation, record imports of foreign steel, federal accountability concerning pollution, lagging productivity and rising labor costs. Plants were relocating, first to southern states and then abroad. Despite these issues, the steel industry is still ingrained in the Cleveland landscape and is not going away. In the 1990s, Cleveland's only major steelmaker still ranked as the third-largest in the country, with 7,000 employees, and was the second-largest non-governmental employer in the city. Significant advances in the steel industry allow Cleveland workers to still compete against cheaper labor from around the world. But it also means that the major steel plants need far fewer employees. The largest current plant has a staff of about 1,900, and this is roughly half its former size. As of 2017, ArcelorMittal is the only remaining steel mill in the industrial valley next to downtown. It began as Corrigan-McKinney Steel Company in 1913, east of the Cuyahoga River in the Industrial Flats. The plant now occupies 950 acres, straddling both sides of the Cuyahoga River. Combine the silhouette of the steel mill, the spread of the fuel tank farms and the giant ore mounds along the river in the industrial valley and the Rust Belt will always influence the vibe and feel of downtown Cleveland. With the lowering of industrial jobs in Cleveland, other jobs have also shrunk in numbers.

The automotive industry has also taken big hits over the last several decades, as foreign car makers have taken huge bites out of the market. Cleveland has a long and storied pedigree in the automobile industry and is experiencing growth at the present time while the rest of the country is seeing auto-based jobs shrink. Automotive employment locally is expected to grow 19 percent to 28,800 employees by 2024. During that same time nationally, automotive employment is expected to decrease by 3 percent. As industry shrank around downtown, a physical void was left on its southern flank along the banks of the Cuyahoga River, and this void would create a barrier to downtown development in that direction.

Retail and service jobs, being dependent on the discretionary income of the workforce, have always followed the currents and eddies of the wages earned in the industrial core. The shopping malls in Cleveland built up to a retail crescendo in the 1970s and 1980s as the suburbs filled out and the factories were flush with workers. The retail world was overbuilt, with strip malls crammed into every spare lot and a large indoor mall around every corner. When the factory jobs moved away, the employment crisis was amplified when store sales started slipping; shopping mall attendance collapsed. Once thriving malls started to empty in the late 1990s. This left acres of empty parking lots and empty desolate storefronts, reflecting a shadow of the midcentury whimsy where shoppers once enjoyed their free time. The pressure on the Cleveland retail industry did not let up when internet shopping further suppressed the brick-and-mortar storefront. Children are now content to stay home and play on their devices or socialize online, and parents can have their goods delivered right to their doorstep.

The first exodus of residents from downtown was in the 1920s and 1930s. People started moving to the outer margins of downtown to get away from the noise, industrial grit and pollution. The interurban trains and the automobile allowed further flight from downtown, and the city center started losing residents. With the first Ford Model T coming out in 1908, the flight to suburbia commenced. By 1925, most of the light rail and trolley routes started converting to buses, and commuting became a normal daily occurrence. To add insult to injury, downtown's crown jewel, the theater district, was dying. The impossibly grand downtown theaters that had been built in the 1920s to fulfil the entertainment needs of the burgeoning industrial town were slowly dwindling away. The theaters never fully recovered after the Great Depression. In the late 1920s, 75 percent of the population was going to the movies.

By the 1970s, these sites were sitting empty and quite literally rotting away. The beautiful grand old single-screen or stage theaters were worn down, painted over or "modernized almost beyond recognition." They could not compete with the suburban malls and their theaters or multiplexes. They fell into disuse in the 1960s and 1970s because of the acceptance of a small piece of technology in everyone's living room called television. Downtown was not thought of as a desirable place to live as long ago as the 1930s. As the 1960s ended, downtown shopping had been abandoned too. The city's growth idled along at a low ebb for the next few decades. City planners and developers worked on ideas to bring Cleveland back from the brink. As the face of Cleveland changed, it became time to start planning a turnaround, and Cleveland took up the call.

HOPE FOR DOWNTOWN

Cleveland was losing people. In the 2000 census, the population of Cleveland was 476,000, and by 2010, it had dropped 17 percent to 396,000. Fortunately since 2010, the population has somewhat stabilized around 385,000 people. This stabilization has hopefully signaled a turnaround in the fortunes of the city.

Suburbs had become king. The development of the suburban shopping mall from the 1970s through the 1990s filled the need to go outside and shop and socialize. With large skylights, flower boxes with exotic greenery and dripping water fountains, the illusion of being outside was simulated for the casual shopper. Cleveland was no different than other large cities across the country, as the suburban shopping mall became a social gathering place for adults and teens. Everything the shopper needed was inside a nice climate-controlled building, with a central food court that never varied from a comfortable seventy-one degrees. There was no need to drive all the way into downtown, and there wasn't anything there anyway. But then the shopping paradigm shifted.

The internet and online shopping happened. With the advent of online shopping and an almost limitless variety of goods available from around the world, shoppers didn't need to leave their houses. There now needs to be a reason to get in one's car, burn expensive gasoline, expose oneself to the elements and visit a brick-and-mortar storefront. Shoppers' expectations changed. Shopping needed to be special. Ironically, it needed to be the way it was in the 1950s. That "motivation" is the shopping, eating and entertainment experience—an experience one cannot get in the home or suburban strip mall around the corner. The experience needs to be enticing, unique and found only in certain locations. People want to feel as if they are going somewhere special. This need has been filled with a new concept of what was commonplace a few generations ago. Retail stores in a conventional setting are vanishing at an astonishing rate. Millennials and empty-nest baby boomers are driving a resurgence in downtown living throughout the country. This type of lifestyle focuses on walkability, a significant shift from the automobile-centric focus of the suburbs.

Enter the regional destination shopping center. They are built from scratch to emulate what is perceived as the ideal and interesting city center. Importantly, there are condominiums and apartments integrated with hotels within the new shopping centers. There is usually at least one shopping arcade, and most of the buildings are built to resemble older-style downtown structures. Fortunately, this blended model of retail and residence aligns with the existing real estate available in downtown Cleveland. The future of residential sustainability is in mixed use, where one can shop, live and work all in one spot. Concerts, spas, fitness clubs and farmers' markets all represent the needs of the new living experience. The innovative malls today look nothing like their predecessors. Open-air living designs go a long way toward lending an atmosphere of a town center.

Downtown Cleveland is uniquely poised to use its real, existing town center to create that desirable, livable, residential shopping experience. Developers have taken note and are leveraging the potential of downtown Cleveland. They are taking strides toward creating a unique, vibrant downtown experience. An important keystone to the future success of downtown Cleveland is creating an attractive residential core of hotels, apartments and condominiums. Loosely defined areas have formed downtown. They are Downtown East, Downtown West, Downtown Central and the Lakefront. The downtown area developers and the city are focusing on these areas to create a residential feel or environment in the immediate downtown area.

This residential development will consist of two components. The first component is desirable housing, and the second is to create what is termed a livable space. A livable space contains entertainment, shopping, green space, convenient grocery stores and restaurants, like what is available in the suburbs. The difference in providing these amenities downtown, as compared to the suburbs, is that they need to be walkable. Fortunately, all this is now happening in downtown Cleveland.

The three demographics driving the walkable living environment are young professionals, millennials and newly retired baby boomers. These groups value the quality of their time over almost anything else. None of them particularly wants to own a car, and all want to have access to most of their needs within a reasonable walk.

There has been significant progress toward creating an inviting walkable environment downtown. Ironically, the desired blend of retail and entertainment venues is very similar to what existed from the 1930s through the 1950s. One used to be able to get a haircut, buy a suit, go to a show and have dinner on a typical midcentury downtown street. This retail formula worked well before the culture of the automobile took hold. The new Eisenhower freeway system freed up travel, broadened the use of cars and helped suppress the need to have everything within walking distance. The buildings that used to provide those services are long gone. They were torn down to make way for the Mall and the new skyscrapers. Fortunately, even better facilities are now being utilized for creating living spaces. Expectations have changed. When one thinks of dining downtown or seeing a show, it is considered a special event. A more upscale environment is expected. Downtown Cleveland is the fastest-growing neighborhood in Northeast Ohio. In 2017, more than seventeen thousand residents lived in downtown Cleveland. Retail investment is creating a welcoming, comfortable place for the day-to-day activities of the inhabitants of downtown—not just a work environment to flee after five o'clock.

The fabulous theaters and Beaux-Arts façades of the old office buildings lend themselves to fulfilling a new ideal of luxury. The buildings are well ornamented, with terrazzo tile, marble floors, statues and metal grills complemented by Art Deco embellishments. Windows in the downtown buildings are large and were designed in the turn of the last century to let in copious amounts of light for the office workers and secretaries. The acres of glass windows now provide great views and lend a modern touch to the older buildings. This type of ornamentation and construction would be cost-prohibitive to include in a modern apartment building today. Cleveland has the unique opportunity to leverage its concentration of remaining vintage real estate into a vibrant and exciting new residential downtown. East of Public Square, popular "districts" have been created, including Nine Twelve, Playhouse Square and the Historic Gateway. West of Public Square are the Warehouse District and East Flats Bank. These areas are still plagued by too many surface lots. There are still many vacant storefronts and empty lots in all the districts offering exciting prospects for future development.

Thousands of new apartments and condominium units have been installed in old office buildings, banks and warehouses, but the condominiums and apartments appearing downtown are not affordably priced for many people. Care must be taken to not outprice downtown housing so as to exclude everyone but the wealthy. Downtown buildings lend themselves to promoting the atmosphere of youthful, upscale living designed for the urban professional or young couple. Fourteen thousand people now live in the city center as opposed to only six thousand in 2002. It is projected that twenty thousand will live in downtown Cleveland by 2020. There are even new hotels being constructed amid the old. The first hotel since 1991 to appear in the downtown area was opened in 2016 near the convention center.

Public Square

Public Square is the heart of downtown Cleveland—the green space where all the districts come together. All the connecting roads meet at Public Square. The completion of the Public Square makeover couldn't have happened at a better time. Public Square now hosts event space, the old Civil War memorial, Centennial Fountain and an ice rink in the winter. The burst in the development of the buildings around Public Square complemented the completion of the new six-and-a-half-acre pedestrian-friendly green space at the hub of the city. The new design routes traffic around the square, allowing only bus traffic down Superior Avenue. There is a free flow of foot traffic between the square's four different sections. Public Square has stood the test of time, and it is one of the very few original parts of the Connecticut Land Company's original plan for the city, created in 1796. The square, with its new makeover, is now properly capable of hosting a wide variety of events year-round.

Tower City resides on the southwestern corner of Public Square. As it returns to relevance, it offers the most unique mix of services in the entire state by providing a casino, a large hotel, retail shops, a theater and office space, all in one massive complex.

The main corridors tying the different districts together include Superior Avenue, Euclid Avenue, East Ninth Street and Ontario Street. All but East Ninth connect to Public Square. The green space provided by the Group Plan Mall also funnels foot traffic between Public Square and the Lakefront. With Public Square ensuring links between the main districts of downtown, economic diversity will be facilitated.

Playhouse Square

Moving forward, Playhouse Square provides a serious cache to the revival of downtown Cleveland. The quality and quantity of its palatial theaters would be impossible to replicate in today's economic environment. Joseph Laronge was a Cleveland real estate mogul who saw Euclid Avenue as a mecca of entertainment and shopping. Without his vision, Euclid Avenue would not have become the great street it was in the 1920s, as well as the district it is now. In 1916, Laronge presented his plan for a theater district in downtown Cleveland. He formed a partnership with Marcus Loew and others to build Playhouse Square over the next five years. Soon after the Ohio and State Theaters were built, Laronge and Loew merged several companies to form Loews Ohio Theatres.

Playhouse Square emerged in 1921–22 with the opening of the State, Ohio, Allen, Palace and Hanna Theaters near the intersection of Euclid Avenue and East Fourteenth Street. Four of the five theaters were interconnected, sharing common lobbies. The largest theater, the

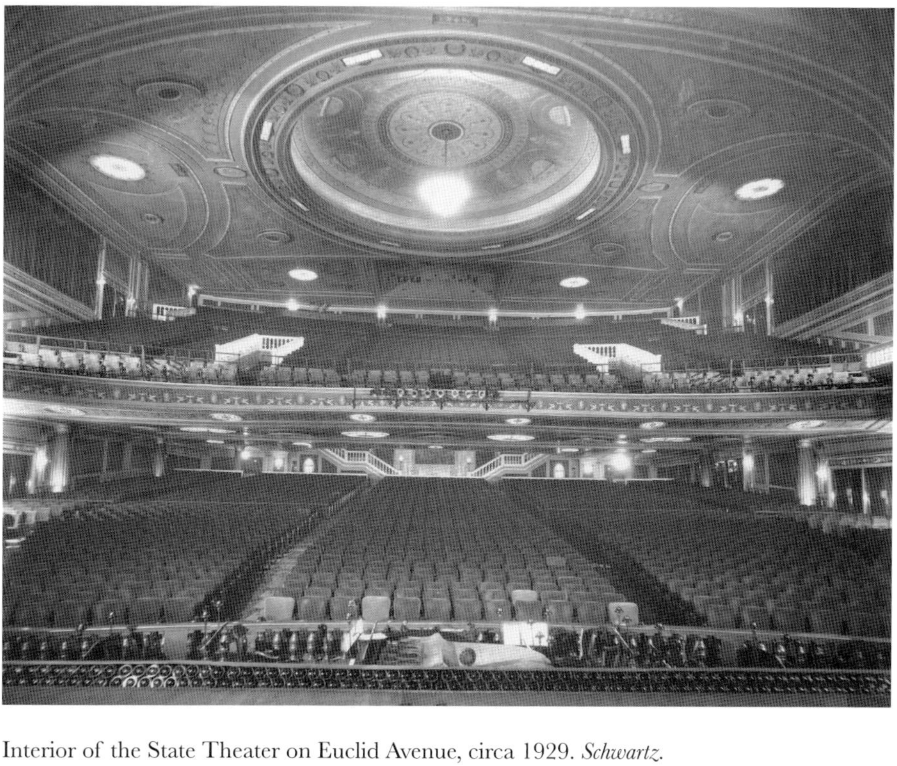

Interior of the State Theater on Euclid Avenue, circa 1929. *Schwartz.*

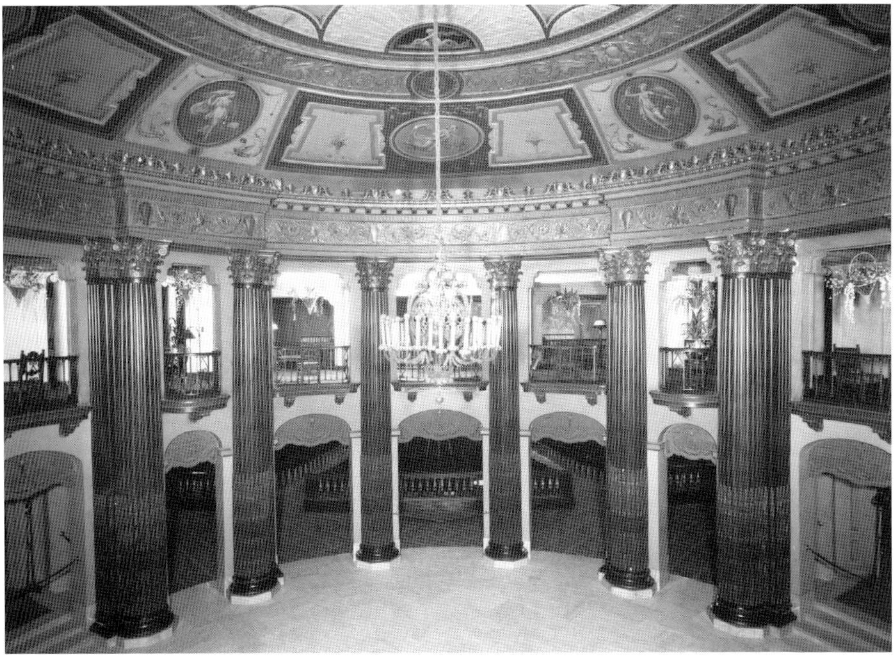

The original Italian Renaissance–style lobby of the Allen Theater, a silent movie house, circa 1929. *Schwartz.*

Palace, was built to host B.F. Keith's vaudeville performances. In addition to vaudeville, the theater district feaured plays, motion pictures and, eventually, Cinerama films. The Depression suppressed attendance at the theaters. By the end of 1969, however, all the theaters but the Hanna had closed due to declining attendance.

Fortunately, most of the downtown theaters survived the wrecking ball, with the Loews Stillman Theater being the exception. The Stillman was torn down to make way for a parking garage. The remaining theaters are enjoying a rebirth and infusion of money. A good example of the commitment toward making the theaters great again is the Loews Ohio, with Playhouse Square's most elaborate lobby, ornamented with a frescoed ceiling, Corinthian columns and three beautiful large murals, all of which were lost to a devastating lobby fire in 1964. About $5 million was dedicated in 2016 to precisely restore the spectacular Neoclassical lobby interior designed by architect Thomas Lamb and built in 1921. Such was the demand for theater in the 1920s that Lamb would end up designing three hundred of the most magnificent theaters across the nation. Playhouse Square as an entity unto itself has seen the completion of $16 million in signage and streetscape improvements at the square. The renovations of the theaters at Playhouse Square bring legitimacy and class to the rebirth of downtown and Euclid Avenue. With its eleven stages and more than ten thousand seats, Playhouse Square now ranks as the second-largest unified arts complex in the United States, after Lincoln Center in New York. There are now also several smaller theaters and the dynamic Idea Center nearby.

Breathing Life into Old Masterpieces

Downtown Cleveland is blessed with an outstanding collection of interesting and beautiful buildings. Most of the buildings appeared during the construction boom of the 1920s and 1930s. This embarrassment of riches allows developers to redefine the neighborhoods and create interesting districts that attract residents back into downtown. The developments are setting standards of reuse that are being used in other large city centers seeking to rejuvenate their downtowns.

Bank buildings are being reused in interesting ways. According to data from the Federal Deposit Insurance Corporation, there were more than 12,000 FDIC-insured institutions at the end of 1995. In 2015, that number stands at just under 6,700. The Cleveland Trust building, erected in 1907, sits at East Ninth Street and Euclid Avenue. It is probably the best example of "thinking outside the box" and reusing a building in downtown Cleveland. One of Cleveland's most venerable banking institutions, the Cleveland Trust Company merged with the Western Reserve Trust Company. The combined offices of this larger bank could not function effectively in ad hoc rented spaces spread around downtown. A competition was declared to design a new headquarters fit for this local institution. Renowned New York architect George Browne Post won the contest. The building remained in the bank's hands until it was shuttered in 1996. The trust building remained closed for almost two decades, a phenomenon not unfamiliar around downtown Cleveland. Large ornate façades fronted with gigantic solid columns supporting classic pediments were a common feature in bank design during the early twentieth century. Banks were a cornerstone for civic life, and people put immense faith and trust in these institutions. With the advent of the office tower, the old solid, elaborate buildings merely became inefficient white elephants in the eyes of most banks. With the renewed interest in living downtown, the old Cleveland Trust building was just waiting for someone with a good idea.

In 2013, the Trust building's attached office tower was converted into apartments, and in 2015, the bank rotunda area was converted into a fine foods grocery. The grocery store also occupies a portion of the connecting Swetland building. The new grocery contains twenty-seven thousand square feet. Surprisingly, it is the first grocery store in downtown Cleveland. This true urban renewal is exactly what is needed to provide the livable environment in a downtown setting. One can move among fluted columns, Corinthian pilasters, bronze doorways and marble floors while judging the freshness of a head of lettuce. Creative mixed-use development of architecturally interesting buildings is proving key to the revitalization of downtown Cleveland. In the case of the corner of Euclid and East Ninth Street, which used to be a financial district with banks on three of four corners, the intersection now has three of its four corners occupied with new residences. A hotel on the corner of East Ninth and Euclid occupies the red pressed brick Schofield Building, which was built in 1902 by Cleveland architect Levi Schofield. The old Union Commerce Bank Building, now called the 925 Building, houses six hundred apartments, a three-hundred-room high-end hotel, 200,000 square feet of retail, a banquet hall, conference space and a lobby open to the public. It can accommodate all these features easily because it contains thirty acres of floor space, second only to the Terminal Tower complex. A very unique feature of the old Commerce Bank Building is a rooftop ticket lobby and waiting room designed for dirigible flights to New York and Chicago. Similar to the dirigible tower on the Empire State Building, the dirigible feature was never used because high winds made landings too difficult. This corner helps anchor the newly formed Nine-Twelve District. This district is located on the eastern side of downtown.

The Standard Building, originally the Brotherhood of Locomotive Engineers Cooperative National Bank Building, is also being converted into residential space. The Standard is another very large ex-bank building sitting on the southwest corner of St. Clair Avenue and Ontario Street. It has three of its four sides covered in cream-colored terra-cotta cladding, with a repeating starburst ornamentation. It was completed in 1925, and at twenty-one stories, it was the second-tallest building in Cleveland at the time. Amazingly, the Brotherhood of Locomotive Engineers and Trainmen, North America's oldest rail union, owned the building up until 2014. Just north of the newly renovated Public Square, the Standard Building may signal the beginning of a new residential district that would be positioned to complement the developments on the east side of Public Square.

The old Board of Education Building, built in 1931 as part of the original Group Plan and located on 1380 East Sixth Street, was converted into a premium hotel in 2016. This building is filled with historic details. When entering the hotel lobby, two Depression-era, WPA-produced murals flank either side of the doorway. The images, titled *Progress of Education* and *The Branches of Education*, await your examination before finding your room.

The massive E-shaped Hotel Cleveland, built in 1918, added residential space and is being repurposed in new and interesting ways. Its proximity to the Quicken Loans Arena, a casino and Public Square make the hotel a key player in the resurgence of downtown. Several other building renovations and reuses are planned or are occurring in downtown Cleveland.

The Lakefront

Cleveland's Lakefront properties are probably the most improved of all the downtown areas over the last one hundred years. That is possibly not a difficult accomplishment when considering that in the 1920s, the Lakefront area was one of the city's garbage dumps and hosted a shantytown during the Depression. It is now divided for planning purposes into the North Coast Harbor, Harbor West and Burke Development Districts. The Lakefront area now hosts an impressive array of world-class attractions. First Energy Stadium, the Great Lakes Science Center and the futuristic Rock and Roll Hall of Fame and Museum, designed by I.M. Pei, are all situated within walking distance of one another. Restaurants, retail arcade, office space and even possible apartments are planned for the area near the Ninth Street Pier north of the Hall of Fame. This development is being carefully vetted and is progressing at a reasonable pace. Green space has been enhanced all around the Lakefront. Wendy Park extends the downtown green space allotment to west of the Cuyahoga River. It is twenty-two acres of tree-lined green space, offering fishing and recreational activities, and it is the only park in the city that provides access to the downtown's Lakefront area. The Lakefront Connector Bridge will link the west bank of the Flats to the Lakefront area. The park was established in 2003.

Other plans are in place to add more connectivity and walkability to the Lakefront area. Once this is accomplished, the recreational aspects of

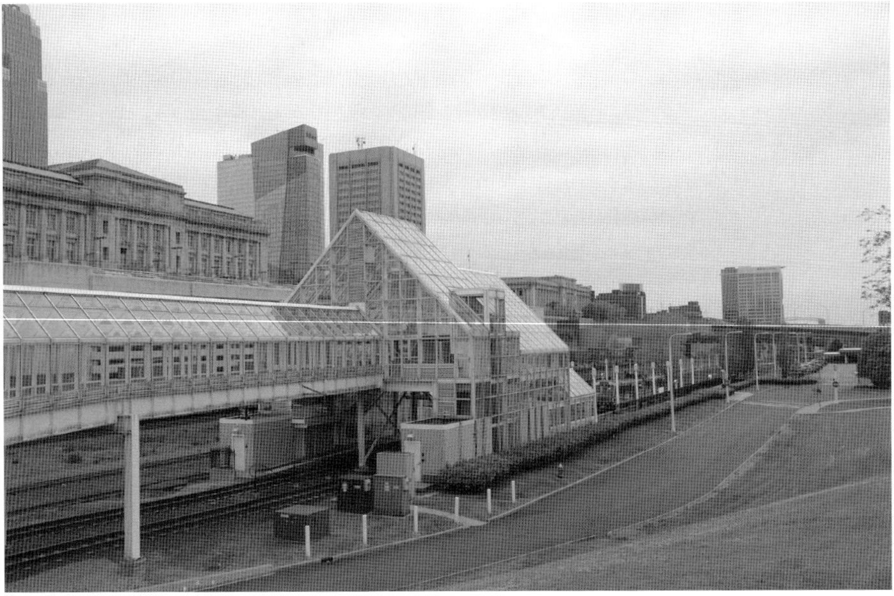

Above: The lakeside rail terminal downtown near Ninth Street and the Rock and Roll Hall of Fame. *Ford.*

Right: The Standard, a newly renovated apartment building on Ontario Street. *Ford.*

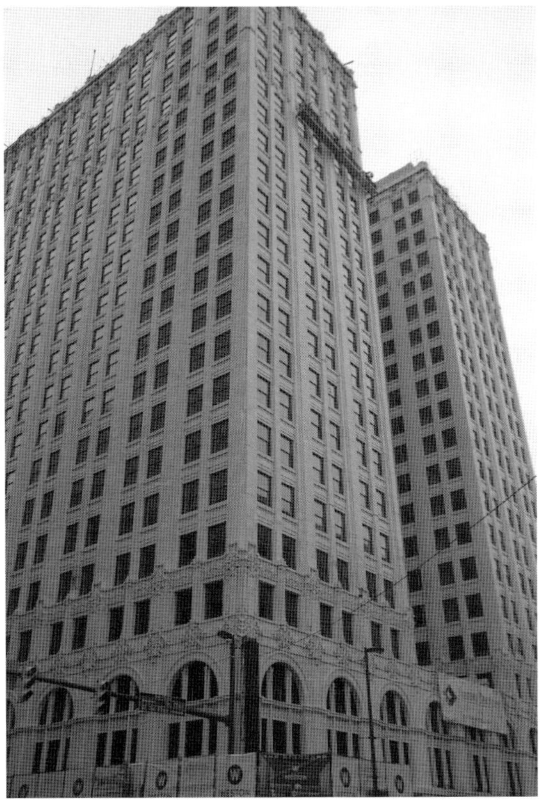

downtown will be greatly enhanced. One of the more ironic changes to the Lakefront area was the building of a rail passenger terminal in 1977 for Amtrak inter-city passenger service. Despite the massive effort by the Van Sweringen brothers to focus the passenger rail through the Tower Terminal, inter-city rail passenger traffic found its way back to the Lakefront. The Lakefront District potential is finally being fully realized and will add a new jewel to the downtown area.

The Public Auditorium and the Convention Center

In the 1920s, Cleveland possessed the much-envied Public Auditorium. The classic Renaissance-style building was designed by city architect J.H. MacDowell, with Frank Walker as consulting architect. The facility was the largest of its kind when it opened in 1922, with a seating capacity of 11,500. The auditorium was heavily used and hosted many high-profile events, such as the Republican National Convention in 1924 and 1936 and two of the American Professional Basketball League national championship games in 1926. Public Auditorium was so advanced architecturally that it became the model for similar public auditoriums in Atlantic City, New Jersey, and Philadelphia, Pennsylvania. There was also exhibition space under the auditorium that was expanded in the 1930s.

By the 1950s, Public Hall was showing its age. The seating arrangement and stage were not conducive to more modern needs. The square footage of convention space available in the auditorium had lost ground to many other cities. There were issues proposed to enhance the convention space in 1957 and 1959 that were rejected. Finally, in 1963, a subterranean addition was approved to expand the space, although this did little to make the auditorium competitive with modern convention facilities.

In 2010, Cuyahoga County purchased the underground convention center west of the auditorium from the city, with the intent to rebuild it. This was done in coordination with the Global Center for Health Innovation, which resides next to the west side of the convention center. A total of 390,000 square feet of meeting space was added to the existing space, along with underground access to the auditorium and a new six-hundred-room adjacent hotel. This was all accomplished while leaving the Mall intact and maintaining the spirit of the original Group Plan. The new convention

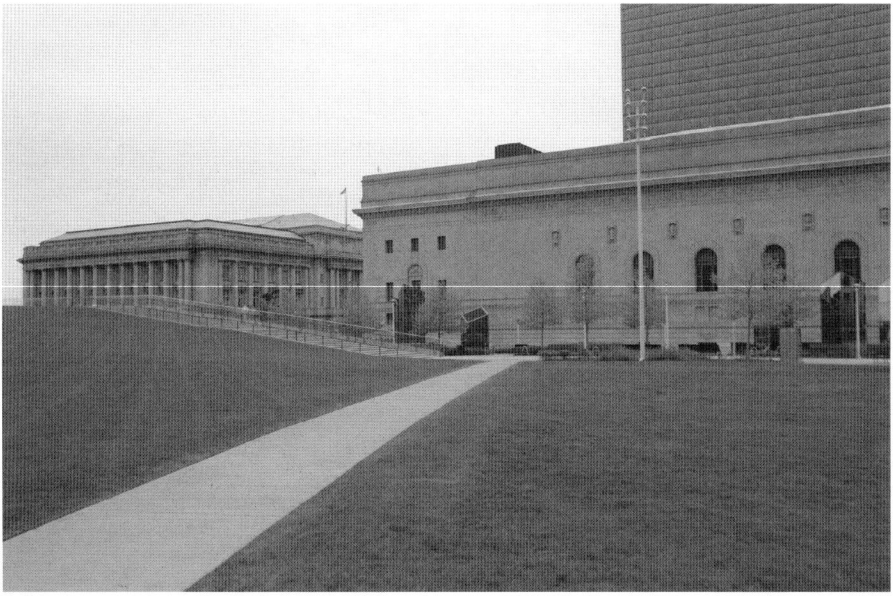

The green grass roof over the convention center. The gently sloping grass hill allows for a street-level entrance to the facility on Lakeside Avenue. *Ford.*

center opened in 2013 and hosted the media center for the 2016 Republican National Convention. In 2016, the convention center hosted nearly 500,000 visitors. The northern end of the Mall—or Mall C, as it is known—was elevated 27 feet above sidewalk level, creating a Lakeside Avenue entrance to the Cleveland Convention Center. This entrance is also used by the Global Center for Health Innovation. Since its 2013 opening, the Global Center for Health Innovation has become a national focal point for healthcare advancements, conventions and industry conferences. The center houses forty-five of the world's leading healthcare brands and hosts more than three hundred industry meetings annually.

These efforts are good examples of the coordinated focus being placed on revitalizing downtown Cleveland. The holistic approach to coordinating the construction of the convention center to pay homage and respect to the old ideals of the Group Plan and incorporate the new buildings around it is what is needed to push downtown Cleveland into the future. The new glass-fronted buildings and the high-tech partners contained within the structures around the convention center will all need to work together to hold on to the solid past of the downtown and hopefully the brilliant future that lies ahead.

Neighborhood Development

Adjacent neighborhoods to downtown are also experiencing a revival, even in building investment. These neighborhoods include Ohio City, Tremont, Glenville and South of Lorain. Development in what is considered the inner city is increasing at different rates in the various neighborhoods. The double-edged sword of gentrification has some longtime residents in these areas concerned that they will be priced out of their homes as property values rise significantly. Cleveland is in the early stages of this real estate upswing. Proponents suggest that the money being poured into the areas will improve the quality of life. There is an urgent need for sensitivity to existing residents, and attention needs to be paid to the needs of each community. A big difference in Cleveland's version of gentrification is that it is more racially diverse than what is occurring on the coasts. The older neighborhoods experiencing new investment don't have the stigma of some of the newer ones that appear to be harder for minorities to gain entry into. The Cleveland neighborhoods that gained the most millennials from 2000 to 2010 also increased in minority population. Growth in Cleveland's inner neighborhoods competes with the efforts in downtown, and development dollars are scarce. One of the more competitive growth areas outside downtown is in the University Circle neighborhood. With Case Western University, galleries and museums, the Circle is experiencing strong growth and investment. A rebirth of downtown Cleveland will be a hollow victory if its neighborhoods are left behind.

A Continued Search for an Identity

Cleveland is adding to its identity as a leader in industry. Once a national leader in industrial patents in the nineteenth century, it has refreshed itself to reflect the high-tech direction the country seems to be heading. In 1946, Cleveland was marketed as being the "Best Location in the Nation" by the Electric Illuminating Company. This concept still applies, if taken literally. Cleveland is within six hundred miles of most of the population of the United States. This is being leveraged now less in an industrial way and more in a high-tech direction. The city is emerging as a biomedical innovation and development center. It has sustained a serious industrial base with its remaining steel and automobile industry factories. Its population has stabilized. It is an exciting time for downtown Cleveland.

The city has aligned organizational resources and committed itself to creating a great downtown. The momentum is there, and the city's existing buildings, parks and attractions are being leveraged to their fullest capacity. In the heart of downtown, ambitious mixed-use urban development will contribute new energy to the city as it turns a corner in its economic and cultural resurgence. Changes in the urban fabric, through the reuse of classic buildings, will make downtown more pedestrian-friendly, and with an influx of new residents, workers and visitors will invigorate the downtown experience. There is still plenty to do to remake Cleveland's downtown into a livable, vibrant community, but the effort is there and well underway. The large gap between the have and have-nots still looms over the city, and the nearly 3 million residents of Greater Cleveland are a diverse lot. They range from Amish woodworkers to newly arrived Middle Easterners. This variety has been a defining feature of Cleveland's past, and its continuance can only help the city move forward as it reinvents itself once again.

Bibliography

Badal, James Jessen. *In the Wake of the Butcher: Cleveland's Torso Murders*. Kent, OH: Kent State University Press, 2014.

Burnham, Daniel H., John M. Carrère and Arnold W. Brunner. *The Group Plan of the Public Buildings of the City of Cleveland*. Report. Chicago: Burnham and Root, 1903.

Case Western Reserve University. *The Cleveland History Timeline*. Encyclopedia of Cleveland History, Case Western Reserve University, 2017. case.edu/ech/timeline.

Cleveland Memory Project. Special Collections Department, Michael Schwartz Library, Cleveland State University.

Hatcher, Harlan. *The Western Reserve: The Story of New Connecticut in Ohio*. 1st ed. Indianapolis: Bobbs-Merrill Company Inc., 1949.

Johannesen, Eric. *Cleveland Architecture, 1876–1976*. Cleveland, OH: Western Reserve Historical Society, 1979.

Lebovitz, Hal. *Best of Hal Lebovitz: Great Sports Writing from Six Decades in Cleveland*. N.p.: Gray & Company, 2006.

Morton, Marian. "It Was the Worst of Times, It Was the Worst of Times: Cleveland and the Great Depression." *Cleveland Digital*, 2015.

Ohio History Connection and the State Library of Ohio. Ohio Memory, 2017. ohiohistorycentral.org.

Pledger, Marcia. "Automotive Industry Employment in Northeast Ohio Expected to Grow in the Next Decade." Cleveland.com, 2014.

———. "Cleveland Steel Goes from Prosperity to Struggles to Pride Again." *Plain Dealer*, 2017.

Richards, George E. "The Last Boy Scout: Eliot Ness' Tenure as Cleveland, Ohio's Public Safety Director." *International Journal of Humanities and Social Science* 1, no. 12 (September 2011): 14.

Richey, Piiparinen. "A Rust Belt Revival Is Beyond Black and White." *Belt Magazine* (2013).

Rosen, Charles. *The Chosen Game: A Jewish Basketball History*. Lincoln: University of Nebraska Press, 2017.

Schwartz, Brad. *The 1936–1937 Great Lakes Exposition*. Charleston, SC: Arcadia Publishing, 2017.

Vieyra, Daniel I., Virginia O. Benson and Robert C. Gaede. *Project: Preservation Cleveland: An Historic and Comparative Analysis*. Cleveland, OH: George Gund Foundation, 1985.

Welland, Sasha S. *A Thousand Miles of Dreams: The Journeys of Two Chinese Sisters*. N.p.: Rowman & Littlefield Publishers, 2007.

Whittlesley, Charles. *Early History of Cleveland Ohio*. Cleveland, OH, 1867.

Index

V

W

About the Authors

Dave Ford has collected many original historic photographs and negatives over the years. He also is an avid World War II and local history buff. He feels that the information contained in historical photos provides a unique, interesting and intimate connection with the past. Ford has made it a priority to restore, digitize and share his collection with others. He has worked with publishers, libraries and private individuals in providing restored photos to be used in books, displays, websites and historical memorials around the country.

Brad Schwartz was born in Cleveland, Ohio, and has resided in Columbus, Ohio, for more than thirty years. He holds a Master of Science degree in urban studies from Cleveland State University's Maxine Goodman Levin College of Urban Affairs and a Master of Landscape Architecture degree from The Ohio State University's Knowlton School of Architecture. He is the author of *The 1936–1937 Great Lakes Exposition* (Arcadia Publishing). Mr. Schwartz and his family live in an 1870s farmhouse that is listed in the U.S. Department of the Interior's National Register of Historic Places.